MW01672604

BAS
ALMANAC

RED-LETTER PRESS, INC.
Saddle River, NJ 07458

*"BASEBALL, IT IS SAID,
IS ONLY A GAME.
TRUE. AND THE GRAND
CANYON IS ONLY A
HOLE IN ARIZONA."*

—George F. Will

DEDICATED TO:

My grandparents, John and Alice Kreismer, who took me to my first game ever- at Yankee Stadium, where the Baltimore Orioles defeated my favorite team, 7-2, on September 26, 1959.

—Jack Kreismer, Publisher

THE BASEBALL ALMANAC

ISBN-10: 0-940462-45-1
ISBN-13: 978-0-940462-45-8

Printed in the United States of America

RED-LETTER PRESS, INC.
P.O. Box 393
Saddle River, NJ 07458
www.Red-LetterPress.com
info@Red-LetterPress.com

THE BASEBALL ALMANAC

EDITORS:

Steve Heldt and Jack Kreismer

CONTRIBUTORS:

Mary Lomio

Eddie Charshafian

Jimmy Charshafian

Jeff Kreismer

David Reyneke

Kobus Reyneke

ACKNOWLEDGMENTS:

Cover design: Behum Graphics

Typography: Christina Chybinski

THE BASEBALL ALMANAC

A Daily Celebration

TODAY'S THOUGHT:

"I believe in the Church of Baseball. I've tried all the major religions and most of the minor ones. And the only church that feeds the soul, day-in day-out, is the Church of Baseball."
—*Annie Savoy,* baseball fan in *Bull Durham*

HISTORY:

On this date in 1943 Negro League star Josh Gibson suffered a nervous breakdown and was sent to the hospital Gibson was released in time for the baseball season, hitting .517 for the year.

BIRTHDAY:

Hank Greenberg, 1911

TRIVIA:

Gibson got his start in the Negro National League in 1930 when he came out of the stands to replace the Homestead Grays starting catcher.

QUIZ:

In what year was the National Negro Baseball League formed:

a) 1900
b) 1910
c) 1920
d) 1930?

ANSWER: *c) 1920*

TODAY'S THOUGHT:

"Baseball: An island of surety in a changing world."—*Bill Veeck*

HISTORY:

On this date in 1986 Bill Veeck, known for his publicity stunts and innovations during his ownership of the Cleveland Indians, St. Louis Browns and Chicago White Sox, died at the age of 71.

BIRTHDAYS:

Bill Madlock, 1951; David Cone, 1963; Edgar Martinez, 1963; Royce Clayton, 1970; Jeff Suppan, 1975

TRIVIA:

In 1951, as a St. Louis owner, Veeck held a "Grandstand Manager's Day", where fans held up placards that said "YES" on one side and "NO" on the other, in response to a publicity director holding up cards with proposed moves, such as "steal", "bunt", or "change pitchers." The fans called an excellent game, as the Browns won, 5-3, and stopped a four-game losing streak.

QUIZ:

As the owner of the Chicago White Sox, Bill Veeck was responsible for giving what well-known major league manager his start in 1979?

ANSWER: *Tony LaRussa*

TODAY'S THOUGHT:

"Trade a player a year too early rather than a year too late."
—*Branch Rickey*

HISTORY:

On this date in 1920 Babe Ruth traded in his red socks for Yankee pinstripes. Boston owner Harry Frazee dealt Ruth to New York to the everlasting dismay of the Red Sox loyalists.

BIRTHDAYS:

Darren Daulton, 1962; A.J. Burnett, 1977

TRIVIA:

Babe Ruth nicknamed his bat "Black Betsy."

EXTRA INNING:

"What impressed me most is that Webb's time was a full two seconds faster than Barry Bonds' home-run trot." –*Scott Osler*, after Alan Webb ran the mile in 3:53:43

QUIZ:

What were Babe Ruth's real first and middle names?

ANSWER: *The Babe was born George Herman Ruth.*

TODAY'S THOUGHT:

"I would always sing *Take Me Out to the Ball Game*, because I think it's the only song I knew the words to!" —*Harry Caray*

HISTORY:

On this date in 1977 Mary Shane was hired by the Chicago White Sox as the first woman TV play-by-play announcer. She teamed up with Harry Caray, Lorn Brown, and Jimmy Piersall for WSNS Channel 44.

BIRTHDAYS:

George Selkirk, 1908; Don McMahon, 1930; Charlie Manuel, 1944; Ted Lilly, 1976

TRIVIA:

Early in his broadcasting career, Harry Caray would sing *Take Me Out to the Ball Game* to himself. Then, in 1976, White Sox owner Bill Veeck secretly placed a public address microphone in the broadcast booth so the entire stadium could hear Caray. When Caray joined the Cubs' broadcast team in 1982, he took the tradition with him.

QUIZ:

Who is credited with writing *Take Me Out to the Ball Game*?

ANSWER: *Jack Norworth - Norworth had never even seen a major league game before writing the song in 1908.*

TODAY'S THOUGHT:

"I'm in the best shape of my life, and that includes my brain."
—*Lenny Dykstra*

HISTORY:

On this date in 2001 Japanese superstar Ichiro Suzuki, who won seven batting titles with the Orix Blue Waves, signed a 3-year, $14 million contract with the Seattle Mariners. The 27-year-old outfielder went on to win the American League's Rookie of the Year and Most Valuable Player Awards.

BIRTHDAYS:

Charlie Hough,1948; Danny Jackson,1962

TRIVIA:

Ichiro finished the 2004 season with 262 hits, breaking the record set by George Sisler of the St. Louis Browns in 1920.

EXTRA INNING:

"Baseball is the blessed silence that comes between Dick Vitale and John Madden." –*Bernie Lincicome*, sports columnist

QUIZ:

Who is the only man to play for both the Seattle Pilots and the Seattle Mariners?

ANSWER: *Pitcher Diego Segui*

TODAY'S THOUGHT:

"I always wanted to be a player, but I never had the talent to make the big leagues. So I did the next best thing: I bought a team."
—*Charlie Finley*

HISTORY:

On this date in 1964 Kansas City owner Charlie Finley signed a two-year agreement to move his Athletics to Louisville, but was denied approval by league owners. The Athletics stayed put in Kansas City until after the 1967 season, when they moved to Oakland.

BIRTHDAYS:

Phil Masi, 1916; Early Wynn, 1920; Ralph Branca, 1926; Norm Charlton, 1963; Marlon Anderson, 1974; Casey Fossum, 1978

TRIVIA:

An aspiring baseball player born in Oakland, California, rap singer MC Hammer was a batboy for the Oakland Athletics. He earned the nickname "Hammer" for his resemblance to "Hammerin' Hank," Henry Aaron.

QUIZ:

The Oakland A's are the last major league team other than the Yankees to win three consecutive World Series titles. In what years did they accomplish this feat?

ANSWER: *1972, '73, & '74*

TODAY'S THOUGHT:

"Ever hear the saying 'There's a fly in my soup?' Well, there was a fly ball in that guy's soup." —*Dave Henderson*, on Cecil Fielder's home run into the centerfield restaurant in the SkyDome

HISTORY:

On this date in 1993 Cecil Fielder signed a then-record 5-year, $36 million contract with the Detroit Tigers. Three years later, he was traded by Detroit to the New York Yankees.

BIRTHDAYS:

Johnny Mize,1913; Alfonso Soriano,1976; Eric Gagne,1976; Francisco Rodriguez,1982

TRIVIA:

In 1992 Fielder became the first player since Babe Ruth to lead the American League in RBI's for three straight years.

EXTRA INNING:

"Is that the best game you ever pitched?" –A media member to Yankees pitcher *Don Larsen*, after his perfect game in the World Series

QUIZ:

In 1947 this baseball Hall of Famer became the only player to hit 50 or more home runs in a season and strike out fewer than 50 times. Name him.

ANSWER: *Johnny Mize, 51 and 42, respectively*

TODAY'S THOUGHT:

"I am the most loyal player money can buy." —*Don Sutton*, pitcher for the Los Angeles Dodgers, Houston Astros, Milwaukee Brewers, Oakland Athletics and California Angels

HISTORY:

On this date in 1996 no one earned the necessary 75 percent in voting by the Baseball Writers Association of America to be elected to the Hall of Fame. Phil Niekro came closest with 68 percent. Two candidates who fell short, Niekro and Don Sutton, would win election to the Hall in 1997 and '98 respectively.

BIRTHDAYS:

Walker Cooper, 1915; Bruce Sutter, 1953; Jason Giambi, 1971; Mike Cameron, 1973; Carl Pavano, 1976; Jeff Francouer, 1984

TRIVIA:

Paul and Lloyd Waner, who played in the outfield together for the Pittsburgh Pirates in the 1920's and '30s, are the only two brothers enshrined in the Baseball Hall of Fame.

QUIZ:

Name the first pitcher to be elected to the Baseball Hall of Fame with a losing record in the majors.

ANSWER: *Satchel Paige, who went 28-31 with the Indians, Browns, and Athletics*

TODAY'S THOUGHT:

"You have to give Pete credit for what he accomplished. He never went to college, and the only book he ever read was *The Pete Rose Story*." —*Karolyn Rose*, Pete's ex-wife

HISTORY:

On this date in 1991 Pete Rose was officially banned from being elected to the Baseball Hall of Fame. Rose would later admit to betting on baseball as the manager of the Cincinnati Reds.

BIRTHDAY:

Otis Nixon, 1959

TRIVIA:

Rose's son, Pete Rose Jr., spent 16 years as a minor league baseball player and had a cup of coffee in the majors.

EXTRA INNING:

"My family was very poor ... It was embarrassing ... When I went bowling, I also had to rent socks." —*Yogi Berra*, about his childhood

QUIZ:

Pete Rose had the most career hits as a switch-hitter. Who's next?

ANSWER: *Eddie Murray with 3,255*

TODAY'S THOUGHT:

"Bruce Sutter has been around for awhile and he's pretty old. He's thirty-five years old. That will give you some idea of how old he is." —*Ron Fairly*, Giants broadcaster

HISTORY:

On this date in 2006 in a special election, seventeen Negro League figures were selected for the Hall of Fame. One of them, Effa Manley, who co-owned the Newark Eagles, became the first woman ever elected to the Hall.

BIRTHDAYS:

Harry Wright, 1835; Jim O'Toole, 1937; Willie McCovey, 1938; Adam Kennedy, 1976; Ervin Santana, 1983

TRIVIA:

Bruce Sutter, also a 2006 inductee, is the first pitcher to be elected to the Hall of Fame who never started a single game in his major league career.

EXTRA INNING:

"We lost 13 straight one year. I decided if we got rained out, we'd have a victory party." –*Lefty Gomez*, on managing in the minors

QUIZ:

Whose names come first and last, alphabetically, among baseball Hall of Famers?

ANSWER: *Hank Aaron and Robin Yount*

TODAY'S THOUGHT:

"I drink after wins, I drink after losses. I drink after rainouts."
—*Bob Lemon*

HISTORY:

On this date in 1999 Mark McGwire's 70th home run ball sold for $3 million, surpassing the mark of $126,500 paid for a Babe Ruth home run ball one year earlier.

BIRTHDAY:

Lloyd McClendon, 1959

TRIVIA:

Carl Yastrzemski's average of .3005 in 1968 was the lowest ever to win the AL batting title.

EXTRA INNING:

"I flush the toilets between innings to keep my wrists strong."
–*John Lowenstein*, on being a DH

QUIZ:

Who are the only two men to play for the Yankees, Dodgers, Giants, and Mets?

ANSWER: *Darryl Strawberry and Jose Vizcaino*

TODAY'S THOUGHT:

"This has been the remarkable thing about the fans in Chicago - they keep drawing an average of a million-three a year, and, when the season's over and they've won their usual seventy-one games, you feel that those fans deserve a medal." —*Harry Caray*, former Cubs broadcaster

HISTORY:

On this date in 1961 owner Phil Wrigley named Charlie Grimm and Verlon Walker to the Chicago Cubs "College of Coaches." He explained that his Cubs would not have a manager for the upcoming season, but rather a "coach of the month."

BIRTHDAYS:

Randy Jones, 1950; Bobby Crosby, 1980; Dontrelle Willis, 1982

TRIVIA:

The bottom of a tombstone in a Chicago area cemetery reads, in Yiddish, "The Cubs stink."

QUIZ:

Who was the first manager to win a pennant in both the National and American Leagues?

ANSWER: *Joe McCarthy, with the Cubs in 1929 and the Yankees in 1932*

TODAY'S THOUGHT:

"If you don't get it by midnight, chances are you ain't gonna get it, and if you do it ain't worth it." —*Casey Stengel*

HISTORY:

On this date in 1982 Henry Aaron and Frank Robinson were elected to the Baseball Hall of Fame. The pair hit a combined 1,341 career homers, yet won only two MVP awards between them (Robinson in 1961 and '66).

BIRTHDAY:

Kevin Mitchell, 1962

TRIVIA:

Hank and Tommie Aaron hit more home runs than any other brother combination in baseball history, 768. Hank hit 755 while Tommie contributed 13.

EXTRA INNING:

"Trying to sneak a pitch past Hank Aaron is like trying to sneak the sunrise past a rooster." —*Joe Adcock*

QUIZ:

Who is the only baseball Hall of Famer whose last name begins with the letter "I"?

ANSWER: *Monte Irvin, who played with the Giants and the Cubs, entered Cooperstown in 1973.*

TODAY'S THOUGHT:

"I don't know if it's good for baseball, but it sure beats the hell out of rooming with Phil Rizzuto!" —*Yogi Berra*, on the marriage of Joe DiMaggio and Marilyn Monroe

HISTORY:

On this date in 1954 Yankee outfielder Joe DiMaggio married American sex symbol and Hollywood actress Marilyn Monroe at San Francisco City Hall. Just 274 days after the wedding, Monroe would file for divorce.

BIRTHDAY:

Sonny Siebert, 1937

TRIVIA:

"Yankee Clipper" Joe DiMaggio played in every inning of every All-Star Game from 1936, his rookie year, through 1942. Joe D is also the first player in professional sports history to be on four championship teams in his first four full seasons.

EXTRA INNING:

"McCovey swings and misses, and it's fouled back." –*Jerry Coleman*

QUIZ:

Of Joe DiMaggio's two brothers, Dom and Vince, which one hit more career home runs?

ANSWER: *Vince, with 125 homers, tops Dom's 87.*

TODAY'S THOUGHT:

"The Dodgers move out of Brooklyn? Impossible."
—*Sports Illustrated*, March 4th, 1957

HISTORY:

On this date in 1957 the Brooklyn Dodgers extended their lease on Ebbets Field for three years. Before the start of the next season, however, owner Walter O'Malley moved the team to Los Angeles, becoming the first major league team to call California home.

BIRTHDAYS:

Bobby Grich, 1949; Delino DeShields, 1969; Matt Holliday, 1980

TRIVIA:

Actor John Forsythe was once the public address announcer for the Brooklyn Dodgers at Ebbets Field.

EXTRA INNING:

"I could never play in New York. The first time I ever came into a game there, I got into the bullpen cart and they told me to lock the door."
–*Mike Flanagan*

QUIZ:

Who was the last man to manage the Brooklyn Dodgers?

ANSWER: *Walter Alston*

TODAY'S THOUGHT:

"A well paid slave is a slave nonetheless." —*Curt Flood*, on baseball's reserve clause

HISTORY:

On this date in 1970 St. Louis outfielder Curt Flood refused a trade to Philadelphia and charged baseball with violating antitrust laws. Although he lost his Supreme Court case, his legal battle opened the doors for free agency.

BIRTHDAYS:

Dizzy Dean, 1910; Jack McDowell, 1966; Ron Villone, 1970; Albert Pujols, 1980

TRIVIA:

In 1988, Curt Flood was named the first (and only) commissioner of the Senior Professional Baseball Association, a league made up primarily of retired ball players. The Senior League was a financial disaster and folded before the end of its second season.

QUIZ:

In 1976, who became the oldest player to get a hit in a major league game?

ANSWER: *White Sox designated hitter Minnie Minoso, at the age of 53*

TODAY'S THOUGHT:

"They invented the All-Star Game for Willie Mays."
—*Ted Williams*

HISTORY:

On this date in 1970 Willie Mays was named *The Sporting News* "Player of the Decade" for the 1960's over Roberto Clemente and Hank Aaron. The "Say Hey Kid" is the all-time leader for putouts by an outfielder with 7,095.

BIRTHDAYS:

Don Zimmer, 1931; Chili Davis, 1960

TRIVIA:

Mays is the first of four men with 500 home runs and 3,000 hits. Others who accomplished this were Hank Aaron, Eddie Murray and Rafael Palmeiro.

EXTRA INNING:

"Every time I look at my pocketbook, I see Jackie Robinson."—*Willie Mays*

QUIZ:

Name the last player to hit home runs in his first two major league at bats.

ANSWER: *Keith McDonald of the St. Louis Cardinals, July 6, 2000.*

TODAY'S THOUGHT:

"Say this for big league baseball - it is beyond any question the greatest conversation piece ever invented." —*Bruce Catton*

HISTORY:

On this date in 1930 Chicago's Art Shires stepped off the field and into the ring to knock out his first boxing opponent, "Mysterious Dan Daly." Shortly after, the White Sox first baseman challenged Hack Wilson to a fight, leading Commissioner Kenesaw Mountain Landis to ban boxing for all baseball players.

BIRTHDAYS:

Curt Flood, 1938; Scott McGregor, 1954; Brady Anderson, 1964; Mike Lieberthal, 1972

TRIVIA:

While in a Philadelphia hotel room in 1929, Shires thought Prohibition agents were raiding him. Although the knock on his door was from Chicago manager Lena Blackburne, Shires punched him for the scare, was suspended, and thus decided to embark on a boxing career.

QUIZ:

This man played for the Dodgers, Cubs, and Celtics, but became better known as a TV star in the 1950's and '60s. Name him.

ANSWER: *Chuck Connors, who starred in the TV Western series The Rifleman.*

TODAY'S THOUGHT:

"I can see how he won 25 games. I can't understand how he lost 5."
—*Yogi Berra*, on Sandy Koufax

HISTORY:

On this date in 1972 Sandy Koufax was elected into the Hall of Fame in his first year of eligibility. At 36, the three-time Cy Young Award winner was the youngest player inducted into the Hall.

BIRTHDAYS:

Chris Sabo, 1962; Phil Nevin, 1971

TRIVIA:

Koufax attended the University of Cincinnati on a basketball scholarship, playing freshman hoops (and baseball) under legendary basketball coach Ed Jucker.

QUIZ:

Which Hall of Fame pitcher did Christy Mathewson defeat for his final major league victory:

a) Mordecai Brown
b) Grover Cleveland Alexander
c) Eppa Rixey
d) Walter Johnson?

ANSWER: *a) Mordecai Brown.... He and Mathewson closed out their careers against each other.*

TODAY'S THOUGHT:

"The greatest untapped reservoir of raw material in the history of our game is the black race." —*Branch Rickey*

HISTORY:

On this date in 1947 Josh Gibson, a star catcher and one of the Negro League's best home run hitters ever, died from a massive stroke at the age of 35. His death came less than twelve weeks before Jackie Robinson broke the color barrier with the Brooklyn Dodgers.

BIRTHDAYS:

Ozzie Guillen, 1964; David Eckstein, 1975

TRIVIA:

Gibson was nicknamed the "Black Babe Ruth." His Hall of Fame plaque says he hit "almost 800" homers in his 17-year career. It is also believed that he recorded a slugging percentage of over 1.000 in two seasons in the late 1930s.

EXTRA INNING:

"No, but he did a lot better than I thought he would." –*Yogi Berra*, on whether Don Mattingly exceeded expectations

QUIZ:

Who was Major League Baseball's second black player, after Jackie Robinson?

ANSWER: *Larry Doby, who debuted with the Indians in 1947.*

TODAY'S THOUGHT:

"The first rule of contract negotiations is don't remind them of what you did in the past - remind them of what you did in the future." —*Stan Musial*

HISTORY:

On this date in 1960, after a sub-par season, Stan Musial surprisingly stated he was overpaid and asked to take a pay cut. His six-figure salary was reduced to $80,000.

BIRTHDAYS:

Johnny Oates, 1946; Brian Giles, 1971; Byun-Hyun Kim, 1979

TRIVIA:

In his 22-year career, Musial batted below .300 only four times, finishing with a career .331 average. Stan the Man won seven batting titles and played in 24 All-Star games, all with the St. Louis Cardinals.

EXTRA INNING:

"Can you believe it? They sent me a whole shipment of bats and not one set of directions." –*Steve Lake*, on hitting .141

QUIZ:

Who was the first player to lead both leagues in home runs? (Hint: It was in the first decade of the 20th century.)

ANSWER: *Sam Crawford, who hit 16 homers for Cincinnati in 1901 and 7 for Detroit in 1908*

TODAY'S THOUGHT:

"Everybody has something to prove each year. Everybody has a responsibility in this game. Even the batboy." —*David Ortiz*

HISTORY:

On this date in 2003 the Boston Red Sox signed utility player David Ortiz, following his release from Minnesota. After earning $170,000 in his first season with the Twins, Ortiz cashed in on a multi-year, multi-million dollar contract with the Sox.

BIRTHDAY:

Chone Figgins, 1978

TRIVIA:

Ortiz hit 20 home runs only once in his six-year career with Minnesota and never had more than 75 RBI's. In his Red Sox career, he's had more than 30 home runs and 100 RBI's in each season he's been with the team.

QUIZ:

What major league team signed David Ortiz as an amateur free agent in 1992?

ANSWER: *The Seattle Mariners. . . He was traded to the Twins in 1996 as a "player to be named later" for Dave Hollins.*

TODAY'S THOUGHT:

"I think I hold the record for most games watched, career."
—*Kurt Bevacqua*

HISTORY:

On this date in 1962 Bob Feller and Jackie Robinson were elected to the Hall of Fame in their first years of eligibility. Feller won 20 games six times, while Robinson, besides breaking the color barrier, led the Dodgers to six pennants in ten years.

BIRTHDAYS:

Kurt Bevacqua, 1947; Mark Wohlers, 1970; Willy Mo Pena, 1982

TRIVIA:

Candlestick Park, former home of the San Francisco Giants, was the site of the last performance of the Beatles, on August 29, 1966.

EXTRA INNING:

"I've been riding on cloud nine since the election, and I don't think I'll ever come down. Today, everything is complete."—*Jackie Robinson*

QUIZ:

What stadium played host to the first major league game on the West Coast?

ANSWER: *Seals Stadium in San Francisco*

TODAY'S THOUGHT:

"You can't just sit on a lead and run a few plays into the line and just kill the clock. You've got to throw the ball over the goddam plate and give the other team a chance." —*Earl Weaver*

HISTORY:

On this date in 1955 the major leagues introduced baseball's equivalent of the shot clock, requiring that pitchers deliver the ball within 20 seconds after taking a pitching position.

BIRTHDAYS:

Rob Dibble, 1964; Scott Kazmir, 1984

TRIVIA:

In an exhibition game between the Yankees and Chattanooga Lookouts in 1931, Babe Ruth and Lou Gehrig were fanned by a 17-year old girl named Jackie Mitchell. Days later, Commissioner Kenesaw Mountain Landis voided Mitchell's contract, claiming baseball was "too strenuous" for women.

EXTRA INNING:

"You wanna be a bat boy? Don't ever do that again." –*Dick Williams*, after his catcher gave the opposing hitter the bat after a foul ball

QUIZ:

By what more popular name do baseball fans know Morganna Roberts?

ANSWER: *The "Kissing Bandit," who hyped her stripper act by running onto the field and kissing ballplayers in the 1970's.*

TODAY'S THOUGHT:

"I signed Oscar Gamble on the advice of my attorney. I no longer have Gamble and I no longer have my attorney." —*Ray Kroc*

HISTORY:

On this date in 1974 the builder of the McDonald's fast-food empire, Ray Kroc, purchased the San Diego Padres for $12 million in cash. Kroc would suffer plenty of indigestion with only one winning season in the ten years he was around to watch the team.

BIRTHDAY:

Derrick Turnbow, 1978

TRIVIA:

US Senator Jim Bunning was the first pitcher to win 100 games in each league in the 20th century. Bunning pitched for the Tigers and Phillies in his major league career.

EXTRA INNING:

"When Sandy Koufax retired." –*Willie Stargell*, on his greatest thrill in baseball

QUIZ:

What player had the most walks in a season without hitting a home run?

ANSWER: *Eddie Stanky, who drew 137 walks for the Brooklyn Dodgers in 1946*

TODAY'S THOUGHT:

"When Neil Armstrong set foot on the moon, he found six baseballs that Jimmie Foxx hit off me in 1937."
—Lefty Gomez

HISTORY:

On this date in 1951 the Baseball Writers Association of America voted Mel Ott and Jimmie Foxx into the Hall of Fame. Both members of the 500 Home Run Club, this was Ott's third year of eligibility and Foxx's fifth.

BIRTHDAY:

Bob Uecker, 1935

TRIVIA:

In 1938, Jimmie Foxx set the major league record for walks in a single game with six.

EXTRA INNING:

"It's like Noah's wife told him- 'Noah, honey, it's going to stop raining one of these days.'" *–Mike Krukow*, on losing a game 21-3

QUIZ:

What player broke Jimmie Foxx's record for the most consecutive seasons with 30 or more home runs?

ANSWER: *Barry Bonds - From 1992 to 2004, 13 seasons, he hit 30 or more homers every year, breaking Foxx's mark of 12, from 1929 to '40.*

TODAY'S THOUGHT:

"The secret of managing is to keep the guys who hate you away from the guys who are undecided." —*Casey Stengel*

HISTORY:

On this date in 1944 Casey Stengel was fired as manager of the Boston Braves after five consecutive losing seasons. Stengel would go on to win seven World Series with the Yankees, become the first manager of the Mets, and be elected to the Hall of Fame in 1966.

BIRTHDAYS:

Phil Plantier, 1969; Angel Berroa, 1978

TRIVIA:

In his major league debut in 1912, Stengel had four singles, a walk and two stolen bases for the Brooklyn Dodgers.

EXTRA INNING:

"Well, I haven't lost a game for a long time." –*Whitey Herzog*, on how he felt about being out of baseball for a year

QUIZ:

During the 1950's, all ten American League pennants were won by teams managed by these two men. Who were they?

ANSWER: *Al Lopez managed Cleveland to the pennant in 1954 and Chicago in 1959. The other eight were won by the Yankees and skipper Casey Stengel.*

TODAY'S THOUGHT:

"Baseball is like driving. It's the one who gets home safely that counts." *—Tommy Lasorda*

HISTORY:

On this date in 1958 Roy Campanella's career ended when a car he was driving in Long Island overturned, leaving him paralyzed from the shoulders down. In his 10 years as the Brooklyn backstop, Campy was the National League MVP three times.

BIRTHDAYS:

George Wright, 1847; Pete Runnels, 1928; Bill White, 1934; Jermaine Dye, 1974; Magglio Ordonez, 1974; Junior Spivey, 1975; Lyle Overbay, 1977

TRIVIA:

In 1950 the Dodgers' Duke Snider, Roy Campanella and Tommy Brown each had a three-home run game during the season. Only two other teams in history have had three players accomplish the feat in one year.

QUIZ:

What stadium was imploded in 2000 despite having $208 million left on its mortgage?

ANSWER: *Seattle's Kingdome*

TODAY'S THOUGHT:

"If my uniform doesn't get dirty, I haven't done anything in the baseball game." —*Rickey Henderson*

HISTORY:

On this date in 1936 the original members of the Baseball Hall of Fame were announced. The first inductees were Ty Cobb, Walter Johnson, Christy Mathewson, Babe Ruth and Honus Wagner. A special committee appointed by Commissioner Kenesaw Mountain Landis made the initial selections.

BIRTHDAYS:

Steve Sax, 1960; Jason Schmidt, 1973

TRIVIA:

Walter Johnson holds the career record for hit batsmen - 2063.

EXTRA INNING:

"Yeah, what paper you write for, Ernie?" –*Yogi Berra*, on being introduced to writer Ernest Hemingway

QUIZ:

The National Baseball Hall of Fame is located in Cooperstown, NY. Where are the professional football and basketball Halls?

ANSWER: *In Canton, OH, and Springfield, MA*

TODAY'S THOUGHT:

"When we win, I'm so happy I eat a lot. When we lose, I'm so depressed, I eat a lot. When we're rained out, I'm so disappointed I eat a lot." —*Tommy Lasorda*

HISTORY:

On this date in 1978 Commissioner Bowie Kuhn cancelled a trade that would have sent pitcher Vida Blue from the Oakland A's to the Cincinnati Reds for first baseman Dave Revering and cash. Believing the A's did not receive enough compensation for Blue, Kuhn overruled the trade.

BIRTHDAYS:

Walt Dropo, 1923; Davey Johnson, 1943; John Patterson, 1978; Jorge Cantu, 1982; Jeremy Hermida, 1984

TRIVIA:

A month later, Oakland got Revering in a different trade, this time for pitcher Doug Bair. Then in March, the A's traded Vida Blue to the San Francisco Giants for seven players and $400,000. Blue went on to win 18 games in 1978.

QUIZ:

In 1965, what Oakland player became the first major leaguer to play an inning at each of the nine defensive positions?

ANSWER: *Bert Campaneris*

TODAY'S THOUGHT:

"It's taken me twenty-seven years and I still don't know why the (knuckle) ball does what it does. If a man asks me how to throw it down and in, I say he's talking to the wrong man."
—*Hoyt Wilhelm*, knuckleball pitcher

HISTORY:

On this date in 2000 Atlanta Braves pitcher John Rocker was suspended by Major League Baseball until May 1 after making racial and ethnic remarks in an interview with *Sports Illustrated*. The southpaw reliever was also fined and forced to attend sensitivity training.

BIRTHDAYS:

Jackie Robinson, 1919; Ernie Banks, 1931; Nolan Ryan, 1947

TRIVIA:

Few people remember Olympian Mack Robinson but many recall his younger brother, baseball pioneer Jackie Robinson.

EXTRA INNING:

"That's more than I expectorated." – Brooklyn Dodger outfielder *Frenchy Bordagaray*, on being fined for $50 for spitting

QUIZ:

What two players have won baseball's Triple Crown twice?

ANSWER: *Ted Williams (1942 & '47) and Rogers Hornsby (1922 & '25)*

TODAY'S THOUGHT:

"One of the beautiful things about baseball is that every once in a while you come into a situation where you want to, and where you have to, reach down and prove something."
—*Nolan Ryan*

HISTORY:

On this date in 1972 Henry Aaron signed a new contract with the Braves, making him the first major league player to earn $200,000 a year. Hammerin' Hank then batted .265 for the season, his lowest season batting average to that point.

BIRTHDAYS:

Paul Blair, 1944; Kent Mercker, 1968

TRIVIA:

The Braves team is the oldest big league franchise in continuous existence today, dating back to the 1870's. They were originally the Cincinnati Red Stockings before a series of moves and name changes brought the club to Atlanta.

EXTRA INNING:

"I've had marriages that didn't last that long." –*Skip Caray*, on an 11-inning game between the Giants and Braves

QUIZ:

Who is the only person to play for the Braves in Boston, Milwaukee, and Atlanta?

ANSWER: *Eddie Mathews, who played for the Braves from 1952-66*

TODAY'S THOUGHT:

"Bad ballplayers make good managers."

—*Earl Weaver*

HISTORY:

On this date in 1876 organized professional baseball began with the formation of the National League. Eight cities agreed to be a part of the National League of Professional Baseball Clubs.

BIRTHDAYS:

Wes Ferrell, 1908; Red Schoendienst, 1923; Scott Erickson, 1968; Melvin Mora, 1972; Mark DeRosa, 1975; Adam Everett, 1977; Jason Vargas, 1983

TRIVIA:

Jim Thorpe is the only man to play in a World Series, win an Olympic gold medal, and be elected to the Pro Football Hall of Fame.

QUIZ:

Four members of the Baseball Hall of Fame have the last name "Robinson." Name them.

ANSWER: *Jackie, Frank, Brooks, and Wilbert (who was inducted as a manager for the Brooklyn Dodgers).*

TODAY'S THOUGHT:

"Connie entered the game when it was a game for roughnecks. He saw it become respectable, he lived to be a symbol of integrity, and he enjoyed every minute of it." —*Sportswriter Red Smith*, on Philadelphia A's owner and manager Connie Mack

HISTORY:

On this date in 1934 the St. Louis Cardinals and St. Louis Browns, in a move to increase attendance, decided to stop broadcasting home games on the radio.

BIRTHDAYS:

Bake McBride, 1949; Fred Lynn, 1952

TRIVIA:

Connie Mack's real name was Cornelius McGillicuddy.

EXTRA INNING:

"All I know is he wasn't carrying a gun." –*Cal Ripken, Sr.*, on riding 21 floors on an elevator with a guy wearing only his socks.

QUIZ:

What pitcher has the dubious distinction of giving up the most home runs in a season?

ANSWER: *Bert Blyleven, 50 in 1986*

TODAY'S THOUGHT:

"I have often called Bowie Kuhn the village idiot. I apologize to all the village idiots of America. He's the nation's idiot."
—*Charles Finley*

HISTORY:

On this date in 1969 Bowie Kuhn was elected Commissioner of Major League Baseball. Kuhn was a compromise choice after a deadlock among supporters of Mike Burke and Chub Feeney.

BIRTHDAY:

Dan Plesac, 1962

TRIVIA:

Kuhn faced tremendous criticism when he announced that the plaques of Negro League players would be in a separate wing of the Baseball Hall of Fame. Complaints from the public ultimately led to the overruling of Kuhn's controversial decision.

QUIZ:

Bowie Kuhn was Major League Baseball's fifth commissioner. Can you name the first four, in order?

ANSWER: *Kenesaw Mountain Landis, Happy Chandler, Ford Frick and William Eckert*

TODAY'S THOUGHT:

"If it wasn't for baseball, I'd either be in the penitentiary or the cemetery." —*Babe Ruth*

HISTORY:

On this date in 1942 the Yankees traded outfielder Tommy Holmes to the Boston Braves. Holmes flourished as a starter for the Braves, compiling a .302 career average.

BIRTHDAYS:

Hank Aaron, 1934; Roberto Alomar, 1968

TRIVIA:

Babe Ruth was a member of the Knights of Columbus.

EXTRA INNING:

"Our similarities are different." –*Dale Berra*, on the comparisons between him and his father

QUIZ:

Two players in major league history have hit pinch-hit home runs in both games of a doubleheader. Name them.

ANSWER: *Joe Cronin, Boston Red Sox, 1943 and Hal Breeden, Montreal Expos, 1973*

TODAY'S THOUGHT:

"The great trouble with baseball today is that most of the players are in the game for the money that's in it - not for the love of it, the excitement of it, the thrill of it." —*Ty Cobb*, in 1925

HISTORY:

On this date in 1958 Ted Williams signed a one-year contract with the Boston Red Sox reported to be worth between $135,000 and $150,000, the highest deal in major league history.

BIRTHDAYS:

Babe Ruth, 1895; Smoky Burgess, 1927; Richie Zisk, 1949; Bob Wickman, 1969

TRIVIA:

Catcher Joe Glenn is the only man to have caught for Babe Ruth and Ted Williams. Glenn caught Ruth during his last pitching outing in 1933, a complete game win. Then, in 1940, he was behind the plate for Williams' lone appearance on the mound, two innings in relief in which he gave up one run.

QUIZ:

True or false? Babe Ruth had over 3,000 career hits.

ANSWER: *False. He had 2,873.*

TODAY'S THOUGHT:

"I found a delivery in my flaw." —*Dan Quisenberry*

HISTORY:

On this date in 1994 the Chicago White Sox signed basketball legend Michael Jordan to a minor league contract. After playing one unproductive season for the Birmingham Barons, Jordan returned to the NBA.

BIRTHDAY:

Dan Quisenberry, 1953

TRIVIA:

Dan Quisenberry led the American League in saves five different years: 1980, 1982, 1983, 1984, and 1985.

EXTRA INNING:

"I used to be the toast of the town. Now I'm the jelly." –*Lloyd Moseby*

QUIZ:

Who's the last pitcher to win the Most Valuable Player award?

ANSWER: *Dennis Eckersley of the Oakland A's in 1992*

TODAY'S THOUGHT:

"Snider, Mantle and Mays - you could get a fat lip in any saloon by starting an argument as to which was best. One point was beyond argument, though. Willie was by all odds the most exciting." —*Red Smith*

HISTORY:

On this date in 1983 Mickey Mantle, one day after becoming the director of sports promotions for the Claridge Hotel and Casino in Atlantic City, was ordered by Bowie Kuhn to cut his ties with Major League Baseball.

BIRTHDAYS:

Fritz Peterson, 1942; Aaron Cook, 1979

TRIVIA:

Mickey Mantle joined Willie Mays as players banned from the game by the commissioner for involvement with legalized gambling. Mays got himself in trouble after joining Bally International as a public greeter and golfer. Both Hall of Famers were later reinstated.

QUIZ:

True or false? Willie Mays never led the National League in batting average for a season.

ANSWER: *False - In 1954, Mays hit .345 to lead the NL.*

TODAY'S THOUGHT:

"Throw peas at their knees and high riders in their eyes. Throw it in here when they're lookin' there, and throw it there when they're lookin' in here." —*Satchel Paige*

HISTORY:

On this date in 1971 Leroy "Satchel" Paige became the first member of the Negro League to be inducted into the Baseball Hall of Fame. Paige played six years in the majors, including a one game appearance for the Kansas City A's in 1965 at the age of 59.

BIRTHDAYS:

Bill Veeck, 1914; John Kruk, 1961; Vladimir Guerrero, 1976

TRIVIA:

Satchel Paige earned his nickname from his job as a redcap at a train station where he carried people's "satchels."

QUIZ:

Name the only person to be enshrined in the National College Football, Pro Football, and Baseball Halls of Fame.

ANSWER: *Cal Hubbard - Hubbard played for Centenary and Geneva Colleges, the New York Giants and Green Bay Packers in the NFL, and was voted into Cooperstown for his work as an American League umpire.*

TODAY'S THOUGHT:

"And the ball is out of here. No, it's not. Yes, it is. No, it's not. What happened?" —*Phil Rizzuto*, New York Yankees announcer

HISTORY:

On this date in 1971 former All-Star first baseman Bill White became the first black announcer in major league history. WPIX-TV hired White to team up with Phil Rizzuto and Frank Messer on New York Yankees broadcasts.

BIRTHDAYS:

Herb Pennock, 1894; Allie Reynolds, 1917; Lenny Dykstra, 1963; Lance Berkman, 1976; Cesar Izturis, 1980

TRIVIA:

From 1989 to 1994, White served as President of the National League, the first African American to do so. That position would be eliminated in both leagues before the 2000 season.

QUIZ:

The annual award given to a broadcaster who has made "major contributions to baseball" is known as what?

ANSWER: *The Ford C. Frick Award, handed out since 1978*

February 11

TODAY'S THOUGHT:

"You hit a four-ounce baseball with a 35-ounce bat and there's going to be some damage." —*George Foster*

HISTORY:

On this date in 2005 Jose Canseco's tell-all book on steroids in baseball, *Juiced*, was released. In the book he writes that sluggers Mark McGwire, Rafael Palmeiro, Juan Gonzalez and Ivan Rodriguez all used illegal performance-enhancing substances.

BIRTHDAY:

Todd Benzinger, 1963

TRIVIA:

Jose Canseco became the first 40-40 player in major league history when he smacked 42 homers and swiped 40 bases for the Oakland A's in 1988.

EXTRA INNING:

"He likes to complain about not playing, which is what he does best- not play." –*Pat Gillick*, on Mike Marshall

QUIZ:

Who was the last player to hit 20 triples in a season?

ANSWER: *Cristian Guzman of the Minnesota Twins in 2000*

TODAY'S THOUGHT:

"The cops picked me up on a street at 3:00 A.M. and fined me $500 for being drunk and $100 for being with the Phillies."

—*Bob Uecker*

HISTORY:

On this date in 2002 Major League Baseball made history when it purchased the Montreal Expos from Jeffrey Loria. Loria sold the Expos for $120 million and then bought the Florida Marlins from John Henry for $158.5 million.

BIRTHDAYS:

Chuck Hafey, 1903; Dom DiMaggio, 1917; Joe Garagiola, 1926

TRIVIA:

Never before had a Major League Baseball team been ownerless during a season. However, between the 1942 and '43 seasons, the National League took over the Philadelphia Phillies from Gerald Nugent, who fell behind in his stadium rent, and sold the team to William D. Cox.

QUIZ:

What owner managed his baseball team for a single game?

ANSWER: *Ted Turner - With his team in the midst of a 16-game losing streak, he managed his Braves in a 2-1 loss to the Pirates. MLB rules do not allow owners to manage, so that was Turner's last game at the helm.*

TODAY'S THOUGHT:

"I'd trip my mother. I'll help her up, brush her off, tell her I'm sorry. But mother don't make it to third." —*Leo Durocher*

HISTORY:

On this date in 1964 Chicago Cubs second baseman Ken Hubbs was killed in a plane crash in Provo, Utah, at the age of 22. Hubbs was the National League Rookie of the Year in 1962.

BIRTHDAY:

Donnie Moore, 1954

TRIVIA:

During his 56-game hitting streak in 1941, Joe DiMaggio hit 56 singles and scored 56 runs.

EXTRA INNING:

"All I'd have to do is make my head look like a slider and he'd miss by six inches." –*Jim Colborn,* on Aurelio Rodriguez threatening to hit him on the head with his bat

QUIZ:

Who was the only man to pinch-hit for Ted Williams?

ANSWER: *Carroll Hardy*

TODAY'S THOUGHT:

"Raise the urinals." —*Darrel Chaney*, on how management could keep the Braves on their toes

HISTORY:

On this date in 1976 the Atlanta Braves sent Valentine's Day cards to their season-ticket holders. After finishing last in their division in 1975, their optimistic card ended with: "Last year's behind us; We're happy to say. Now we're tied for first, Happy Valentine's Day." They would again finish in last place in '76.

BIRTHDAYS:

Dave Dravecky, 1956; Kelly Stinnett, 1970; Damso Marte, 1975; Brad Halsey, 1981

TRIVIA:

The Atlanta Braves won the NL East every year from 1991 to 2005, with the exception of the strike-shortened '94 season. They had only one World Series title in 1995, however, to show for their efforts.

QUIZ:

In what other sport did Atlanta Braves' owner Ted Turner capture a championship?

ANSWER: *Yachting - Turner's yacht "Courageous" won the America's Cup in 1977.*

TODAY'S THOUGHT:

"When I began playing the game, baseball was as gentlemanly as a kick in the crotch." —*Ty Cobb*

HISTORY:

On this date in 1990 the Major League Baseball owners refused to open spring training without a new Basic Agreement with the Players' Association. This began a lockout that would last 32 days and delay the start of the season by a week.

BIRTHDAY:

Ugueth Urbina, 1974

TRIVIA:

Brady Anderson set a record for homering from both sides of the plate in the same game when he did it four times in 1996.

EXTRA INNING:

"When Charlie Finley had his heart operation, it took eight hours- seven just to find his heart." –*Steve McCatty*

QUIZ:

Who hit more home runs in his 40's than any other player?

ANSWER: *Carlton Fisk - He played six more years with the Chicago White Sox after he turned 40 and hit 72 home runs during those six seasons.*

TODAY'S THOUGHT:

"Therapy can be a good thing; it can be therapeutic."
—*Alex Rodriguez*, on the benefits of seeing a therapist

HISTORY:

On this date in 2004 the Yankees and Rangers traded infielders. The Bronx Bombers sent second baseman Alfonso Soriano to Texas for shortstop Alex Rodriguez and his twenty-five million dollar a year contract. Rodriguez agreed to change his infield position, taking his Gold Glove to third base.

BIRTHDAYS:

Billy Hamilton, 1866; Eric Byrnes, 1976

TRIVIA:

According to an old Metropolitan Life study, baseball players live significantly longer than the average male - especially third basemen.

EXTRA INNING:

"We got a guy on our club who has such bad hands, his glove is embarrassed." –*Frank Sullivan*

QUIZ:

Name the only second baseman in major league history to win back-to-back MVP awards.

ANSWER: *Joe Morgan of the Cincinnati Reds earned the MVP in 1975 and '76.*

February 17

TODAY'S THOUGHT:

"A baseball manager is a necessary evil."
—*Sparky Anderson*

HISTORY:

On this date in 1995 Detroit Tigers manager Sparky Anderson was put on an involuntary leave of absence when he refused to manage replacement players in a spring training game. The Baltimore Orioles also announced that they would not play games against teams using replacement players.

BIRTHDAYS:

Scott Williamson, 1976; Josh Willingham, 1979

TRIVIA:

Sparky earned the nickname "Captain Hook" because of his tendency to pull under-performing pitchers from the game early.

EXTRA INNING:

"If I tell, everybody will do it, and we'll be out there for five hours, but nobody will get anybody out." –*Rick Dempsey*, on not giving the secret to his hitting secret

QUIZ:

Who was the last starter to go 15 innings in a game?

ANSWER: *Gaylord Perry lasted 15 innings for the Cleveland Indians in 1974 against the Milwaukee Brewers. Perry gave up four runs and struck out 14 batters.*

TODAY'S THOUGHT:

"Baseball is like a church. Many attend, but few understand."
—*Wes Westrum*

HISTORY:

On this date in 1967 NBC-TV, which scheduled a charity softball game between celebrities and major leaguers, snuck Eddie Feigner, the country's premier fast-pitch softball pitcher, onto the celebrity team. Feigner embarrassed baseball's best, striking out the likes of Willie Mays, Roberto Clemente, and Harmon Killebrew.

BIRTHDAYS:

Kevin Tapani, 1964; Shawn Estes, 1973; Alex Rios, 1981

TRIVIA:

Eddie Feigner began touring the country in 1946, playing with just three other players. His team, the King and His Court, regularly beat nine-man softball squads. In 1999, *Sports Illustrated* named the King and His Court as its eighth favorite all-time sports team.

QUIZ:

True or false? At one time foul balls (except bunts or tips) were not counted as strikes.

ANSWER: *True, until the early 1900's*

TODAY'S THOUGHT:

"Sometimes in this game it's as good to be lucky as it is to be good." —*Vida Blue*

HISTORY:

On this date in 1987 pitcher Vida Blue announced his retirement from baseball, one month after signing a contract with Oakland. Blue won 209 games in his 17-year career and a Cy Young Award in 1971.

BIRTHDAY:

Dave Stewart, 1957

TRIVIA:

Vida Blue, like Ichiro Suzuki, wore his first name on the back of his baseball jersey.

EXTRA INNING:

"The advantage of playing in New York is getting to watch Reggie Jackson play every day. And the disadvantage is in getting to watch Reggie Jackson play every day." –*Graig Nettles*

QUIZ:

Who were the four 20-game winners for the 1971 Baltimore Orioles?

ANSWER: *Jim Palmer, Dave McNally, Mike Cuellar and Pat Dobson*

TODAY'S THOUGHT:

"Cardinal rule for all hitters with two strikes on them: Never trust the umpire!" —*Robert Smith*

HISTORY:

On this date in 1966 the American League announced the hiring of Emmett Ashford to become the first black umpire in major league history. Ashford had already become the first professional black umpire exactly 15 years earlier, in the Southwestern International League.

BIRTHDAYS:

Sam Rice, 1890; Tommy Henrich, 1913; Shane Spencer, 1972; Livan Hernandez, 1975; Justin Verlander, 1983; Brian McCann, 1984

TRIVIA:

Sportscaster Brent Musburger was a baseball umpire in the Midwest League in 1959. His broadcasting career started ten years later, when he joined WBBM Radio in Chicago as sports director.

QUIZ:

This major league umpire, turned author, wrote books titled *The Umpire Strikes Back* and *The Fall of the Roman Umpire* in the 1980's. Name him.

ANSWER: *Ron Luciano*

TODAY'S THOUGHT:

"God gets you to the plate, but once you're there you're on your own." —*Ted Williams*

HISTORY:

On this date in 1969 Ted Williams returned to baseball, signing a five year contract to manage the Washington Senators. Williams was named American League Manager of the Year after he led the franchise to its best record ever.

BIRTHDAYS:

Tom Yawkey, 1903; Alan Trammell, 1958

TRIVIA:

Fenway Park in Boston has a secret message on the "Green Monster." The initials of the Red Sox late owners, Thomas and Jean Yawkey, are inscribed on it in Morse code.

EXTRA INNING:

"One thing you can learn as a Cubs fan: when you buy your tickets, you can bank on seeing the bottom of the ninth." —*Joe Garagiola*

QUIZ:

What is the record for most at bats in a major league game without a hit?

ANSWER: *Eleven - Charles Pick of the Boston Braves went 0-11 in a 26-inning game against the Brooklyn Dodgers in 1920.*

TODAY'S THOUGHT:

"As I remember it, the bases were loaded." — *Phillies center fielder Garry Maddox*, on his first big league grand slam

HISTORY:

On this date in 2004 former Phillies catcher Andy Seminick, the last living everyday player from the Whiz Kids, died at the age of 83. In 1950, he and other members of a youthful Philadelphia team shocked everyone by winning the National League pennant.

BIRTHDAYS:

Sparky Anderson, 1934; Steve Barber, 1938; Kazuhiro Sasaki, 1968; J.J. Putz, 1977; Casey Kotchman, 1983

TRIVIA:

In 1949, the Phillies tied a major league record by hitting five home runs in a single inning. Seminick hit two home runs in that eighth inning, and collected a total of three in the game.

QUIZ:

The 1983 Philadelphia Phillies veteran team was sometimes referred to by what name?

ANSWER: *The Wheeze Kids, because of the advanced ages of many of the club's best players*

TODAY'S THOUGHT:

"He's a better interview from the left side than the right side."
—*Al Michaels*, joking about an interview with the switch-hitting Bobby Bonilla

HISTORY:

On this date in 1960 a wrecking ball painted to resemble a baseball reduced Ebbets Fields to rubble, three years after the Dodgers packed up and headed west. The stadium opened in 1913.

BIRTHDAYS:

Elston Howard, 1929; Bobby Bonilla, 1963

TRIVIA:

Elston Howard and Pee Wee Reese have the distinction of playing on the most losing World Series teams. Both were on the short end of the stick six times in their careers.

EXTRA INNING:

"Yeah, only in America can a thing like this happen." –*Yogi Berra*, on a Jewish mayor being elected in Dublin, Ireland

QUIZ:

Who was the first Los Angeles hurler to pitch a no-hitter at Dodger Stadium?

ANSWER: *Bo Belinsky of the Los Angeles Angels, in 1962*

TODAY'S THOUGHT:

"I was thinking of making a comeback, until I pulled a muscle vacuuming." —*Johnny Bench*

HISTORY:

On this date in 1990 Tony Conigliaro died at the age of 45 of pneumonia and kidney failure. After being hit in the face by a pitch in 1967, he came back to hit 36 HRs in 1970, but was slowed by a vision problem and never returned to form.

BIRTHDAYS:

Honus Wagner, 1874; Eddie Murray, 1956; Mike Lowell, 1974; Bronson Arroyo, 1977

TRIVIA:

Conigliaro holds the MLB record for most home runs (25) hit by a teenage player. At the age of 22, he became the youngest American League player to hit 100 career home runs.

QUIZ:

What pitcher beaned Conigliaro in 1967?

ANSWER: *The Angels' Jack Hamilton hit Conigliaro on his left cheekbone, resulting in severe damage to his left retina.*

TODAY'S THOUGHT:

"Baseball is a ballet without music. Drama without words.A carnival without kewpie dolls." —*Ernie Harwell*, broadcaster

HISTORY:

On this day in 2002 84 year-old Tigers broadcaster Ernie Harwell announced he would retire at the end of the year The Hall of Famer spent 62 years at the microphone in New York and Detroit.

BIRTHDAYS:

Monte Irvin, 1919; Ron Santo, 1940; Paul O'Neill, 1963

TRIVIA:

Former pitcher Tommy John had a doorbell, which played *Take Me Out to the Ball Game.*

EXTRA INNING:

"Because 85 percent of the fans have artificial hips." –*Robin Ventura*, on why Bo Jackson received a standing ovation in a spring training game in Sarasota, Florida

QUIZ:

In 1986, '87 and '88, the Rookie of the Year Award was won by members of the Oakland A's. Who were they?

ANSWER: *Jose Canseco*, 1986; *Mark McGwire*, 1987; *Walt Weiss*, 1988

TODAY'S THOUGHT:

"It's a good thing Babe Ruth isn't here. If he was, George Steinbrenner would have him bat seventh and say he's overweight." —*Graig Nettles*

HISTORY:

On this date in 1935 the New York Yankees released Babe Ruth, allowing him to sign a $20,000 contract with the Boston Braves. In 1934, Ruth had one of his worst seasons as a Yankee with a .288 batting average, 22 home runs and 84 RBIs.

BIRTHDAYS:

Grover Cleveland Alexander, 1887; J.T. Snow, 1968; Josh Towers, 1977; Gary Majewski, 1980

TRIVIA:

In 1914, as a 19-year old, Ruth signed a contract with the Baltimore Orioles of the International League. Because he was not yet a legal adult, Orioles owner Jack Dunn became Ruth's guardian. That spring training, he acquired the nickname Babe when teammates referred to him as "Dunn's baby."

QUIZ:

In what two states do major league teams play their spring training games?

ANSWER: *Florida and Arizona*

TODAY'S THOUGHT:

"If horses don't eat it, I don't want to play on it." —*Dick Allen*, on artificial turf

HISTORY:

On this date in 1973 the salary bar was raised again. Dick Allen signed a three-year deal for $250,000 a year with the Chicago White Sox, making him the highest paid player in major league history.

BIRTHDAY:

Matt Stairs, 1968

TRIVIA:

The first team to hold spring training in Arizona was the Detroit Tigers in 1929.

EXTRA INNING:

"He doesn't drink, he doesn't smoke, he doesn't chew, he doesn't stay out late, and he still only hits .250." –*Casey Stengel*, on Bobby Richardson

QUIZ:

The Giants, Indians, and Pirates each lost 100 or more games in 1985. One player spent a portion of the season with each team. Who was it?

ANSWER: *Johnnie LeMaster played for the Giants (62-100), Indians (60-102), and Pirates (57-104).*

TODAY'S THOUGHT:

"I won't say that women belong in the kitchen, but they don't belong in the dugout." —*Mets broadcaster Keith Hernandez,* upon seeing a female member of the Padres training staff in the dugout

HISTORY:

On this date in 1986 Commissioner Peter Ueberroth handed seven major leaguers one-year drug-related suspensions without pay. Among the victims were the Mets' Keith Hernandez and Yankees' Dale Berra.

BIRTHDAY:

Frank Malzone, 1930

TRIVIA:

Keith Hernandez holds the career record for game-winning RBIs, a statistic that was official only from 1980 to '88, with 129. He also holds the single-season record, 24, set in 1985.

EXTRA INNING:

"He takes a bunt for a called third strike." –*Ron Fairly*

QUIZ:

From 1988 to 1990 the NL RBI crown was won by three members of the Giants. Name this trio.

ANSWER: *Will Clark, Kevin Mitchell and Matt Williams were the respective leaders in those years.*

TODAY'S THOUGHT:

"It doesn't matter if his shoulder's sore. He doesn't throw anyone out anyway." —*Sparky Anderson*, on Kirk Gibson having one assist in 298 chances in 1985

HISTORY:

On this date in 2000 Sparky Anderson, Bid McPhee and Negro League slugger Norman Stearnes were elected to the Baseball Hall of Fame by the Veterans Committee.

BIRTHDAY:

Pepper Martin, 1904; Al Rosen, 1924

TRIVIA:

Sparky Anderson's first name is George.

EXTRA INNING:

"We forgot about the Canadian exchange rate, so it's really an 82 mph." –*Mike Flanagan*, on Mike Boddicker's fastball being clocked at 88 mph against the Blue Jays

QUIZ:

Who managed the most games without ever finishing in first place?

ANSWER: *Jimmy Dykes, who in 22 seasons managed 2,962 games and never finished higher than third*

TODAY'S THOUGHT:

"I owe my success to expansion pitching, a short right field fence and my hollow bats." —*Norm Cash*

HISTORY:

On this date in 1993 New York Yankees owner George Steinbrenner was reinstated by Major League Baseball. He had been suspended by Commissioner Fay Vincent for his relationship with Howie Spira, a convicted gambler.

BIRTHDAY:

Harry Caray, 1914

TRIVIA:

Harry's son, Skip Caray, and his grandson, Chip, both became broadcasters. Chip replaced Harry after he died in 1998. He was the Cubs broadcaster until 2004 when he went to Atlanta to join his father, Skip, in calling Braves games.

QUIZ:

What Hall of Fame shortstop/outfielder had the most hits during the decade of the '80's?

ANSWER: *Robin Yount, 1,731*

TODAY'S THOUGHT:

"A life isn't significant except for its impact on other lives."
—*Jackie Robinson*

HISTORY:

On this date in 2005 Jackie Robinson was posthumously awarded the Congressional Gold Medal, the highest national tribute for accomplishment.

BIRTHDAYS:

Mel Ott, 1909; Terry Steinbach, 1962; Ron Gant, 1965; Jay Gibbons, 1977

TRIVIA:

In 1941, Jackie Robinson became the first athlete in the history of UCLA to letter in four sports (baseball, football, basketball and track) in the same year.

EXTRA INNING:

"Never has a home run been so anonymous." –*Steve Garvey*, on hitting a home run while an attractive woman was parading around the stands

QUIZ:

Who were the first two black managers to face each other in a regular season game?

ANSWER: *In 1989, the Orioles' Frank Robinson faced off against the Blue Jays' Cito Gaston. Baltimore won, 16-6.*

TODAY'S THOUGHT:

"We're fine. The only time we lose our concentration is when the umpire says, 'Play ball'" —*Lou Piniella*, when asked if his team was mentally prepared

HISTORY:

On this date in 1988 the first black player in the American League, Larry Doby, was elected to the Baseball Hall of Fame. Doby began his career in 1947 with the Cleveland Indians.

BIRTHDAY:

Jorge Julio, 1979

TRIVIA:

Not only was Doby the second black player in the big leagues, he was also the second black manager after Frank Robinson. Doby became manager of the White Sox in 1978.

EXTRA INNING:

"I always said I gave Mike Cuellar more chances than I gave my first wife."
–*Earl Weaver*

QUIZ:

What two Hall of Famers were traded for each other in 1930?

ANSWER: *Heinie Manush of the St. Louis Browns was traded to the Washington Senators for Goose Goslin, who hit 30 homers for the Browns that season.*

TODAY'S THOUGHT:

"I always felt the more Browns that I could place on other teams, the better off I'd be." —*Bill Veeck*, then owner of the inept St. Louis Browns

HISTORY:

On this date in 1950 the St. Louis Browns, hoping to change their losing ways, hired psychologist Dave Tracy. He hypnotized the team to instill a winning mentality. However, Tracy eventually got fed up and stated that the Browns suffered from "loser's syndrome."

BIRTHDAYS:

Jeff Pfeffer, 1888; Dazzy Vance, 1891; Lefty O'Doul, 1897

TRIVIA:

The 1944 World Series was played by teams from the same city and the same park. The St. Louis Browns faced the St. Louis Cardinals at Sportsman's Park. This would be the Browns' only Fall Classic, losing to the Cardinals, four games to two.

QUIZ:

What major league franchise was formerly known as the Spiders?

ANSWER: *The Cleveland Indians*

TODAY'S THOUGHT:

"The redhead is so careful of the truth, he uses it sparingly."
—*Dan Parker* on Larry MacPhail

HISTORY:

On this date in 1966 Marvin Miller was elected executive director of the Major League Players Association. At the time, Miller was the assistant to the president of the United Steelworkers Union.

BIRTHDAYS:

Brian Hunter, 1971; Paul Konerko, 1976; Eric Bedard, 1979

TRIVIA:

One-time Brooklyn Dodgers president Larry MacPhail served as an artillery captain in France and Belgium during World War I.

EXTRA INNING:

"The Dodgers are such a .500 club, they could probably split a three-game series." –*Vin Scully*

QUIZ:

Who was the first Little Leaguer to play in the big leagues?

ANSWER: *Joey Jay, in 1954*

TODAY'S THOUGHT:

"I want all the kids to do what I do, to look up to me. I want all the kids to copulate me." —*Andre Dawson*

HISTORY:

On this date in 1987 Expos' free agent Andre Dawson, disgusted that he was being offered only $1 million by Montreal, offered to sign a "blank check" contract with Chicago. The Cubs wound up signing Dawson to a one-year contract worth $500,000.

BIRTHDAYS:

Lefty Grove, 1900; Willie Stargell, 1940; Marcus Thames, 1977; Clint Barmes, 1979

TRIVIA:

Dawson once paid a $1,000 fine for a tantrum he threw after being called out on strikes. He wrote a check with the notation, "Donation for the blind."

QUIZ:

What two outfielders each won three consecutive Gold Gloves in the 1990's as members of the Pirates?

ANSWER: *Barry Bonds and Andy Van Slyke*

TODAY'S THOUGHT:

"When I leave this game, I'd rather be respected than loved."
—*Jeff Kent*

HISTORY:

On this date in 1999 the Baltimore Orioles announced they would go to Cuba later that month to play an exhibition game against the Cuban national team. It was the first time in 40 years that an American professional team played a game there.

BIRTHDAYS:

Joe Carter, 1960; Jeff Kent, 1968

TRIVIA:

Jeff Kent is the all-time leader for home runs by a second baseman.

QUIZ:

What Cuban-born player won batting titles in his first two years in the big leagues?

ANSWER: *Tony Oliva of the Twins in 1964 and '65*

TODAY'S THOUGHT:

"Haven't they suffered enough?" —*Beano Cook*, after Commissioner Bowie Kuhn gave the fifty-two former Iran hostages lifetime Major League Baseball passes

HISTORY:

On this date in 1941 Phillies pitcher Hugh Mulcahy became the first major leaguer to be drafted into the armed forces. Mulcahy led the league in defeats in two of the three seasons before he left.

BIRTHDAYS:

Pete Fox, 1909; Carl Furillo, 1922; Jim Bouton, 1939; Dick Allen, 1942; Jim Rice, 1953; Ryan Freel, 1976; Juan Encarnacion, 1976

TRIVIA:

While over 100 big leaguers were involved in World War II, only two, Elmer Gedeon and Harry O'Neill, were killed.

QUIZ:

What Hall of Fame pitcher died in 1925 from tuberculosis he had contracted after being exposed to poisonous gas during World War I?

ANSWER: *Christy Mathewson*

TODAY'S THOUGHT:

"McCovey swings and misses, and it's fouled back."
—Jerry Coleman

HISTORY:

On this date in 1995 Major League Baseball approved two expansion teams, the Arizona Diamondbacks and Tampa Bay Devil Rays. They would begin play in 1998.

BIRTHDAYS:

Jackie Jensen, 1927; Terry Mulholland, 1963; Benito Santiago, 1956; Aaron Boone, 1973

TRIVIA:

Aaron Boone hit a home run in the 11th inning of game seven of the ALCS against the Boston Red Sox to send the New York Yankees to the 2003 World Series. He joined Bill Mazeroski and Joe Carter as the only players to hit walk-off homers to end a postseason series.

QUIZ:

How many World Series sweeps have the Yankees enjoyed?

ANSWER: *Eight - The Yankees swept the World Series in 1927, 1928, 1932, 1938, 1939, 1950, 1998, and 1999.*

TODAY'S THOUGHT:

"Playing baseball for a living is like having a license to steal."
—*Pete Rose*

HISTORY:

On this date in 1963 rookie second baseman Pete Rose made his debut for the Cincinnati Reds, doubling twice in an exhibition game against the Chicago White Sox.

BIRTHDAYS:

Steve Howe, 1958; Mike Timlin, 1966

TRIVIA:

Long before he got into big trouble for tax evasion, Pete Rose got into a little trouble for parking illegally outside Cincinnati's Riverfront Stadium. The street name on the ticket? Pete Rose Way.

EXTRA INNING:

"Now he can relate to the reporters who have interviewed him." –*Bret Lewis* of KFWB radio in Los Angeles on the news of Barry Bonds' root canal surgery

QUIZ:

With what team did Pete Rose get his 4,000th hit?

ANSWER: *The Montreal Expos, in 1984*

TODAY'S THOUGHT:

"A second-guesser is one who don't know anything about the first guess, and he's one who needs two guesses to get one right." —*Tommy Lasorda*

HISTORY:

On this date in 2004 in the first game ever played at Petco Park, the San Diego Padres' new home, a record was set for the best attended game in college baseball history as 40,106 fans saw Tony Gwynn's San Diego State Aztecs shut out the University of Hawaii, 4-0.

BIRTHDAYS:

Dock Ellis, 1945; Cesar Geronimo, 1948; Bobby Abreau, 1974

TRIVIA:

In 1997, San Diego State's baseball facility was renamed Tony Gwynn Stadium.

QUIZ:

He was the victim of Bill Mazeroski's 1960 World Series home run, who redeemed himself with a 1-0, seventh-game victory over the Giants in the 1962 Series. Name him.

ANSWER: *Ralph Terry of the Yankees*

TODAY'S THOUGHT:

"It's what you learn after you know it all that counts."
—*Orioles manager Earl Weaver*

HISTORY:

On this date in 1921 Commissioner Kenesaw Mountain Landis suspended eight members of the Chicago White Sox, including Joe Jackson, for their alleged involvement in the fixing of the 1919 World Series. Although they would later be acquitted by a jury, Landis banned the Black Sox for life.

BIRTHDAYS:

Johnny Callison, 1939; Jimmy Wynn, 1942; Dale Murphy, 1956; Darryl Strawberry, 1962; Steve Finley, 1965; Raul Mondesi, 1971

TRIVIA:

Shoeless Joe Jackson got his nickname when he played without his cleats in a minor league game. Suffering from a blister from one of his new spikes, he played in his stockings. When he reached base, a heckler called him a "shoeless son-of-a-bitch."

QUIZ:

Who's the only catcher to win a home run title?

ANSWER: *Johnny Bench, 1970 and 1972*

TODAY'S THOUGHT:

"People ask me what I do in winter when there's no baseball. I'll tell you what I do: I stare out the window and wait for spring."
—*Rogers Hornsby*

HISTORY:

On this date in 1954 Braves starting outfielder Bobby Thomson fractured his ankle during an exhibition game, opening a spot in the lineup for a 20-year-old rookie named Henry Aaron.

BIRTHDAYS:

Frank "Home Run" Baker, 1886; Will Clark, 1964; Johan Santana, 1979

TRIVIA:

Hank Aaron won the NL home run crown four times. Three of the four times, he finished the year with 44 homers - the number on his uniform.

EXTRA INNING:

"His limitations are limitless." –Phillies manager *Danny Ozark*, on Mike Anderson

QUIZ:

True or false? Willie Mays never hit a home run in the World Series.

ANSWER: *True*

TODAY'S THOUGHT:

"It took me 17 years to get 3,000 hits. I did it in one afternoon on the golf course." —*Hank Aaron*

HISTORY:

On this date in 1954 Hank Aaron made his first spring training start for the Milwaukee Braves in an exhibition game against the Boston Red Sox. Aaron recorded three hits, including a home run. In his rookie year, Aaron hit .280 with 13 home runs and 58 RBI's.

BIRTHDAYS:

Kirby Puckett, 1961; Kevin Brown, 1965; Bobby Jenks, 1981

TRIVIA:

Hank Aaron finished his career with 3,771 hits, meaning if you subtracted every single one of his 755 homers from his total, he would still have accumulated over 3,000 hits.

EXTRA INNING:

"I watch a lot of baseball on the radio." –*Gerald R. Ford*

QUIZ:

How many major league players have hit 600 or more career home runs?

ANSWER: *Four - Hank Aaron, Barry Bonds, Babe Ruth, Willie Mays*

TODAY'S THOUGHT:

"There have been only two geniuses in the world - Willie Mays and Willie Shakespeare." —*Tallulah Bankhead*, actress

HISTORY:

On this date in 1885 a lower court in New York ruled that playing baseball on Sunday is a crime.

BIRTHDAYS:

Bobby Bonds, 1946; Harold Baines, 1959

TRIVIA:

Bobby Bonds was the first player to have two consecutive seasons of 30 home runs and 30 stolen bases. In 1977, Bonds hit 37 homers and stole 41 bases. He then hit 31 dingers while pilfering 43 bases in 1978.

EXTRA INNING:

"When I played baseball, I got death threats all the time – from my mother."
–*Bob Uecker*

QUIZ:

Who holds the record for most consecutive years leading the league in stolen bases?

ANSWER: *Luis Aparicio. Aparicio led the American League in stolen bases for 9 straight seasons from 1956 to 1964.*

TODAY'S THOUGHT:

"I was the worst hitter ever. I never even broke a bat until last year. That was backing out of the garage."

—Hall of Fame pitcher Lefty Gomez

HISTORY:

On this date in 1972 twenty-two year-old Athletics pitcher Vida Blue announced his rejection of the team's contract offer and said he would retire to go work for a toilet fixture company. Blue eventually came to terms with Oakland and began his season in May. A 24-game winner in 1971, Blue would have a disappointing 6-10 record in '72.

BIRTHDAYS:

Buddy Myer, 1904; Lloyd Waner, 1906; Hee Sop Choi, 1979; Curtis Granderson, 1981

TRIVIA:

Vida Blue is the last switch hitter to win the American League MVP award, in 1971. Obviously, it wasn't for his .118 batting average, but rather for his 24-8 record, 1.82 ERA and 301 strikeouts that year.

QUIZ:

A major league starting pitcher must work at least how many innings to get credit for a victory?

ANSWER: *Five*

TODAY'S THOUGHT:

"For the Washington Senators, the worst time of the year is baseball season." —*Sportswriter Roger Kahn*

HISTORY:

On this date in 1965 Jackie Robinson signed a contract with ABC-TV to become a member of their baseball broadcast team. He was the first black broadcaster to receive a network position.

BIRTHDAY:

Bill Mueller, 1971

TRIVIA:

In 1956 Robinson was traded to the New York Giants for Dick Littlefield and $30,000. However, he retired instead of reporting to the team.

EXTRA INNING:

"The only thing standing between Jack Perconte and an outstanding major league career is performance." –*Del Crandall*

QUIZ:

In 2001, Alex Rodriguez hit 52 home runs, the most ever by a shortstop. Who's second?

ANSWER: *Ernie Banks, 47, in 1958*

TODAY'S THOUGHT:

"That's his style of hitting. If you can't imitate him, don't copy him." —*Yogi Berra*

HISTORY:

On this date in 1987 Oklahoma State's Robin Ventura began a remarkable hitting streak where he would go on to hit safely in 58 consecutive games. His streak ended May 29, when Stanford held him hitless in a College World Series game.

BIRTHDAYS:

Scott Podsednik, 1976; Fernando Rodney, 1977; Chad Cordero, 1982

TRIVIA:

While Ventura may have passed Joe DiMaggio's major league mark, Joltin' Joe made some history himself before his big league days. As an 18-year old, he hit safely in 61 straight games for the San Francisco Seals of the Pacific Coast League in 1933.

QUIZ:

When the Chicago White Sox drafted Robin Ventura, he became teammates with the man who ended his college streak. Name this Stanford pitcher.

ANSWER: *Jack McDowell*

TODAY'S THOUGHT:

"If I had my choice between a pennant and a triple crown, I'll take a pennant every time." —*Carl Yastrzemski*

HISTORY:

On this date in 1961 the Boston Red Sox announced that a rookie named Carl Yastrzemski would start in left field. Yaz filled the shoes of Hall of Famer Ted Williams, responding with a career that would place him in the Hall in 1989.

BIRTHDAYS:

Richie Ashburn, 1927; Jason LaRue, 1974

TRIVIA:

Yaz retired from the Red Sox after 23 seasons at age 44. No one else had a longer career with one team.

QUIZ:

I had more major league at-bats before the age of 25 than any other player in history. Who am I?

ANSWER: *Robin Yount, who joined the Brewers in 1974 at age 18*

TODAY'S THOUGHT:

"I want to be remembered as a ballplayer who gave all he had to give." —*Roberto Clemente*

HISTORY:

On this date in 1973 Roberto Clemente was elected to the Baseball Hall of Fame. Clemente's induction came less than three months after his death in a plane crash while delivering relief supplies to earthquake victims in Nicaragua.

BIRTHDAY:

George Altman, 1933

TRIVIA:

Roberto Clemente doubled off the Mets' Jon Matlack on September 30, 1972, in the final game of the regular season, earning his 3,000th career hit. The last game Clemente ever played was at Cincinnati's Riverfront Stadium in the 5th game of the '72 NLCS, a 4-3 loss to the Reds.

QUIZ:

Only one other time in history has baseball relaxed its rule requiring five years of inactivity for entrance to the Hall of Fame. What player was the exception made for?

ANSWER: *Lou Gehrig, in 1939- the expectation was that he would not survive the five-year wait due to his illness.*

TODAY'S THOUGHT:

"Your Holiness, I'm Joseph Medwick. I too used to be a Cardinal." —*Joe Medwick*, former St. Louis Cardinal

HISTORY:

On this date in 1975 Joe Medwick died at the age of 63. One of the most feared hitters as a member of the "Gashouse Gang" in the '30's, Medwick hit 205 home runs and had a .324 batting average over his 17-year career.

BIRTHDAYS:

Shawon Dunston, 1963; Cristian Guzman, 1978

TRIVIA:

Fenway Park's Green Monster is 37 feet high.

EXTRA INNING:

"The more I played with them, the more I found that no one could take a joke- my batting average." –*Rocky Bridges*, on batting .237 for the Dodgers

QUIZ:

In 1956 one player in each league hit 50 or more home runs. Can you name either of them?

ANSWER: *Mickey Mantle hit 52 for the Yankees; Duke Snider hit 53 for the Dodgers*

TODAY'S THOUGHT:

"Statistics are like a bikini; they show a lot but not everything."

—Lou Piniella

HISTORY:

On this date in 1991 at Sotheby's in New York, a 1910 tobacco card of Hall of Fame shortstop Honus Wagner was purchased by hockey legend Wayne Gretzky and LA Kings owner Bruce McNall for $451,000.

BIRTHDAYS:

Billy Goodman, 1926; Glenallen Hill, 1965; Cory Lidle, 1972

TRIVIA:

The Honus Wagner tobacco card is known as the "Mona Lisa of Baseball Cards" due to its rarity and legend. Wagner objected that his name be used in association with smoking. The American Tobacco Company stopped production of his card, but approximately 50 were still released.

QUIZ:

With what team did Honus Wagner begin his major league career?

ANSWER: *The Louisville Colonels, in 1897*

TODAY'S THOUGHT:

"I don't know a lot about politics, but I know a lot about baseball."
—*Richard Nixon*

HISTORY:

On this date in 1962 William DeWitt bought the Cincinnati Reds from the Crosley Foundation for $4.265 million. DeWitt had served as club president under Powel Crosley, Jr. before the owner's death in 1961.

BIRTHDAYS:

Lee May, 1943; Mike Remlinger, 1966; Ramon Ortiz, 1973; Mark Buerhle, 1979

TRIVIA:

Lee May hit the last home run at Crosley Field on June 24, 1970.

QUIZ:

Which left-handed batter hit four consecutive homers in a game:

a) Bobby Murcer
b) Ted Williams
c) Lou Gehrig
d) Babe Ruth?

ANSWER: *c) Lou Gehrig, in 1932*

TODAY'S THOUGHT:

"Your life or mine?" —*Whitey Herzog*, Cards manager, on being offered a lifetime contract by 80-year-old Gussie Busch

HISTORY:

On this date in 1911 St. Louis Cardinals' president Stanley Robison died unexpectedly. He left the club to his niece, Helene Hathaway Britton, who immediately became the first female owner of a Major League Baseball team. Britton sold the team in 1916.

BIRTHDAYS:

George Sisler, 1893; Bruce Hurst, 1958; Wilson Alvarez, 1970; Steve Karsay, 1972

TRIVIA:

In 1984, the Cardinals retired the uniform number 85 for then-owner August "Gussie" Busch, in honor of his age. The club was purchased by the Anheuser-Busch brewery in 1953 and sold in 1996, six years after Busch's death.

QUIZ:

In 2006, the St. Louis Cardinals moved into their new Busch Stadium, which replaced Busch Memorial Stadium, their home since 1966. Where did the franchise play before that?

ANSWER: *Sportsman's Park (which was renamed Busch Stadium in 1953)*

TODAY'S THOUGHT:

"This is the best time of the year. Heck, once the season starts, I got to go to work." —*Brooks Robinson*

HISTORY:

On this date in 2001 Randy Johnson killed a dove when the bird flew in front of his 95-mph fastball during a spring training game.

BIRTHDAYS:

Lee Mazzilli, 1955; Tom Glavine, 1966; Travis Fryman 1969; Dan Wilson, 1969

TRIVIA:

Baseball's 1991 Cy Young Award winner Tom Glavine was a 1984 fourth round pick of the NHL's Los Angeles Kings.

QUIZ:

How many home dates did it take for the Rockies to break the one-million mark in attendance in their first season:

a) 17
b) 27
c) 37
d) 47?

ANSWER: *a) 17 games in 1993 - The Rockies broke the major league record set by the Blue Jays one year earlier.*

TODAY'S THOUGHT:

"Carrots might be good for my eyes, but they won't straighten out the curveball." —*Carl Furillo*

HISTORY:

On this date in 1951 in an exhibition game at the University of Southern California, 19-year old Mickey Mantle smashed a home run estimated at 660 feet. The shot cleared USC's Bovard Field and then went the width of a practice football field before landing.

BIRTHDAY:

Jose Vizcaino, 1968

TRIVIA:

Mantle, born in the Depression Era in 1931, was named after his father Mutt's favorite player, Mickey Cochrane, a Hall of Fame catcher who played with the A's and Tigers.

QUIZ:

Mickey Mantle has hit the most home runs in World Series history, 18. Who is second?

ANSWER: *Babe Ruth, with 15*

TODAY'S THOUGHT:

"Sometimes they write what I say and not what I mean."
—*Pedro Guerrero*, on sports writers

HISTORY:

On this date in 1989 *Sports Illustrated* published a story about Cincinnati Reds manager Pete Rose's gambling activities. Rose would be banned for life from Major League Baseball as a result of betting on the game.

BIRTHDAY:

Miller Huggins, 1878

TRIVIA:

The Dowd Report asserted that Rose bet on 52 Reds games in 1987, wagering a minimum of $10,000 a day.

QUIZ:

My cup of coffee in the major leagues lasted one year, but it was a good one. I was named *The Sporting News* NL Rookie Pitcher of the Year and I pitched a scoreless ninth inning in the final game of the 1961 World Series. Who am I?

ANSWER: *Ken Hunt, who went 9-10 for the Reds during the regular season*

TODAY'S THOUGHT:

"He's a pitcher, part yogi and part recluse. Impressively liberated from our opulent life-style, Sidd's deciding about yoga —and his future in baseball." —*George Plimpton*, in his fake *Sports Illustrated* article (The first letters of those words spell out "Happy April Fools Day.")

HISTORY:

On this date in 1913 the St. Louis Browns made an unusual trade when they sent infielder Buzzy Wares to a minor league team in exchange for the rental of a stadium. The Montgomery Black Sox allowed the Browns to use their stadium during spring training, rent-free.

BIRTHDAYS:

Lon Warneke, 1909; Paul Wilson, 1973

TRIVIA:

A 1985 issue of *Sports Illustrated* contained a fictitious article about Mets pitching prospect Sidd Finch, who threw a 168-mph fastball. In this April Fools article, author George Plimpton tricked readers by making up quotes from real Mets players and staging several photos.

QUIZ:

The Mets moved to Shea Stadium in their third year. Where did they play during their first two seasons?

ANSWER: *The Polo Grounds*

TODAY'S THOUGHT:

"It's a partial sellout." *—Braves broadcaster Skip Carey,* at a game that drew only 6,000 fans

HISTORY:

On this date in 1983 the Los Angeles Dodgers became the first team to cut off season ticket sales before opening day. With 27,000 tickets sold, the Dodgers wanted their fans to be able to buy tickets to individual games.

BIRTHDAYS:

Cy Young, 1867; Denny McLain, 1944; Brian Jordan, 1967; Danny Kolb 1975

TRIVIA:

Cy Young threw the first perfect game in American League history when he led the Boston Red Sox over Connie Mack and the Philadelphia Athletics in 1890.

EXTRA INNING:

"I hate the minor leagues. I'd rather go out to lunch with my ex-wife's attorney than play in the minors." *–Dave Collins*

QUIZ:

Of the original sixteen teams from 1901, which is the only one that hasn't sent an outfielder to the Hall of Fame?

ANSWER: *The Chicago White Sox*

TODAY'S THOUGHT:

"None of my committee members are up for trade. Our team is clicking on all cylinders, and I know how trades can turn out. I'm the one who traded Sammy Sosa to the Chicago White Sox!" —*President George W. Bush*, former owner of the Texas Rangers

HISTORY:

On this date in 1992 the Chicago Cubs acquired outfielder Sammy Sosa and pitcher Ken Patterson from the Chicago White Sox for outfielder George Bell. Bell's career would last only two more seasons, while Sosa would become an All-Star and hit over 500 career home runs.

BIRTHDAYS:

George Van Haltren, 1866; Grady Little, 1950

TRIVIA:

When Sammy Sosa hit his 500th career home run in 2003, he became the 18th member of that club, and the first Latin American, to reach the magic number.

QUIZ:

When was the last year the Chicago Cubs won the World Series?

ANSWER: 1908 - *They haven't been to a Fall Classic since 1945.*

TODAY'S THOUGHT:

"You may go a long time without winning, but you never forget that scent." —*Steve Busby*, 70-54 in eight years in the majors

HISTORY:

On this day in 1998 the Tampa Bay Devil Rays and the Arizona Diamondbacks made their official major league debuts. The Devil Rays fell to Detroit, 11-6, before the home fans, while Colorado spoiled the Diamondbacks' home opener, 7-2.

BIRTHDAYS:

Tom Evers, 1852; Chien Ming Wang, 1980

TRIVIA:

Wade Boggs hit the first home run in Tampa Bay history, while Travis Lee hit Arizona's initial round-tripper.

QUIZ:

In what year did the Boston Braves play their final game in Boston:

a) 1941
b) 1952
c) 1960
d) 1971?

ANSWER: *b) 1952*

TODAY'S THOUGHT:

"Trying to hit him is like trying to eat Jello with chopsticks."
—*Bobby Murcer*, on Phil Niekro

HISTORY:

On this date in 1970 the bankrupt Seattle Pilots were purchased by a group led by Milwaukee businessman Bud Selig. Tickets for the Milwaukee Brewers' home games went on sale the next day.

BIRTHDAYS:

Phil Niekro, 1939; Rusty Staub, 1944

TRIVIA:

Pitcher Joe Niekro hit only one home run in his big league career. It came off his brother, Phil.

EXTRA INNING:

"He looks less comfortable donning a glove than anyone since O.J."
–*Steve Rushin* of *Sports Illustrated*, on Dodgers outfielder Bobby Bonilla

QUIZ:

On July 22, 2006, in a 5-4 New York victory over Toronto, Alex Rodriguez of the Yankees earned a golden sombrero. What did he do?

ANSWER: *He struck out four times.*

TODAY'S THOUGHT:

"I'm rich. What am I supposed to do, hide it?" —*Lou Whitaker*, arriving in a stretch limo for a players' union meeting during the 1994 strike

HISTORY:

On this date in 1995 the longest work stoppage in professional sports history came to an end. After 234 total days and 275 cancelled games, baseball's owners accepted the players' offer to return to work.

BIRTHDAYS:

Tommy Bond, 1856; Hugh Jennings, 1869; Luke Appling, 1907; Billy Pierce, 1927; Don Sutton, 1945; Reggie Smith, 1945; Jon Lieber, 1970

TRIVIA:

On Opening Day in 1995, three men wearing T-shirts with the word "Greed" leaped onto the field at Shea Stadium and threw dollar bills at players. In Cincinnati, one fan paid for a plane to fly over Riverfront Stadium that pulled a sign reading, "Players and Owners - To Hell With You!"

QUIZ:

What MLB player became the first to make one million dollars in a single season?

ANSWER: *Nolan Ryan, who signed with the Houston Astros in 1980 for three years*

TODAY'S THOUGHT:

"Of all major team sports, baseball alone acknowledges perfect games in its record book." —*Good Reading* magazine

HISTORY:

On this date in 1985 players and owners agreed to expand the League Championship Series from its best-of-five games format to best-of-seven.

BIRTHDAYS:

Wally Moon, 1930; Gary Pettis, 1958; Mike Lansing, 1968

TRIVIA:

Rotisserie baseball was cooked up by inventor Daniel Okrent in 1980.

EXTRA INNING:

"Just to have his body, I'd trade mine and my wife's and throw in some cash." –*Pete Rose*, on Mike Schmidt

QUIZ:

Who has the most Gold Glove Awards among players not in the Hall of Fame?

ANSWER: *Jim Kaat -Kaat won 16 Gold Gloves as a pitcher during his career.*

TODAY'S THOUGHT:

"I never doubted my ability, but when you hear all your life you're inferior, it makes you wonder if the other guys have something you've never seen before. If they do, I'm still looking for it." —*Hank Aaron*

HISTORY:

On this date in 1974 Hank Aaron, on his very first swing of the season, hit home run number 714 off Cincinnati's Jack Billingham to tie Babe Ruth's career mark.

BIRTHDAYS:

Tris Speaker, 1888; Joe Vosmik, 1910; Gil Hodges, 1924; Jim Fregosi, 1942; Scott Rolen, 1975

TRIVIA:

Another historic Opening Day occurred on this date in 1988 when Toronto's George Bell became the first man in baseball history to hit three home runs in the first game of the season. Bret Saberhagen and the Royals were the victims in the Blue Jays' 5-3 win.

QUIZ:

In 1968, baseball's Opening Day was postponed five days due to what unfortunate occurrence?

ANSWER: *The assassination of Dr. Martin Luther King, Jr.*

TODAY'S THOUGHT:

"Baseball was, is, and always will be the best game in the world." —*Babe Ruth*

HISTORY:

On this date in 1982 Jim Kaat pitched one inning in the St. Louis Cardinals' season opener. Although that appearance was brief, it marked the 24th straight year that Kaat had played major league ball, a record at the time.

BIRTHDAYS:

Ron Hansen, 1938; Rennie Stennett, 1951; Brandon Backe, 1978

TRIVIA:

Kaat retired after twenty-five straight years in the big leagues. His mark was surpassed only by Tommy John (26 years) and Nolan Ryan (27 years).

EXTRA INNING:

"I've seen guys pitch bad, and I've seen guys pitch in bad luck, but you've done an outstanding job of putting it all together." –*Sparky Lyle*, to Jim Kern

QUIZ:

Who hit the first World Series home run in Yankee Stadium?

ANSWER: *Casey Stengel hit an inside-the-park home run to break a ninth-inning tie, giving the Giants a 5-4 win over the Yankees in game one of the 1923 World Series.*

TODAY'S THOUGHT:

"I screwed up the game of baseball. Baseball needed a jolt of offense for attendance, so they decided on the DH. I never thought it would last this long." —*Ron Blomberg*

HISTORY:

On this date in 1973 Ron Blomberg of the New York Yankees became the first designated hitter in major league history. In his first plate appearance, Blomberg walked with the bases loaded off Luis Tiant. The Red Sox won the game, 15-5.

BIRTHDAYS:

Mickey Cochrane, 1903; Ernie Lombardi, 1908; Bert Blyleven, 1951; Bret Boone, 1969; Andy Phillips, 1977

TRIVIA:

In 1997, San Francisco Giants outfielder Glenallen Hill became the first National League player to DH in a regular-season game. The game marked the inaugural game in interleague play, as the Giants faced the Texas Rangers at The Ballpark at Arlington.

QUIZ:

In 1978 this Detroit Tiger became the first player to appear as a designated hitter in all 162 games. Who was it?

ANSWER: *Rusty Staub*

TODAY'S THOUGHT:

"There has only been one manager, and his name is John McGraw."

—Connie Mack

HISTORY:

On this date in 1979 Ken Forsch of the Houston Astros gave the hometown fans something to cheer about, hurling a no-hitter against Atlanta. Forsch's 6-0 win was the only no-hitter tossed in the majors that year.

BIRTHDAY:

John McGraw, 1873; Bobby Doerr, 1918; Brett Tomko, 1973; Ron Belliard, 1975; Adrian Beltre, 1979

TRIVIA:

Ken's brother, Bob, pitched a no-hitter in 1978, making them the first siblings to pitch no-hitters. Bob Forsch also pitched another no-no for St. Louis in 1983, blanking Montreal, 3-0.

QUIZ:

Besides the expansion teams of the '90's, only two major league clubs have never had a pitcher throw a no-hitter. Name them.

ANSWER: *The New York Mets and San Diego Padres*

TODAY'S THOUGHT:

"The pitcher has got only a ball, I've got the bat. So the percentage in weapons is in my favor and I let the fellow with the ball do the fretting." —*Henry Aaron*

HISTORY:

On this date in 1974 Hank Aaron hit a 1-0 pitch off Al Downing into the left field bullpen for career home run 715, breaking the record held by Babe Ruth since 1935.

BIRTHDAYS:

Catfish Hunter, 1946; Gary Carter, 1954; Alex S. Gonzalez, 1973; Timo Perez, 1975; Felix Hernandez, 1986

TRIVIA:

When he was chasing the Babe's career home run record, Henry Aaron often avoided attention by registering at hotels under the alias George Ruth.

QUIZ:

Who holds the major league record for most consecutive innings played?

ANSWER: *Cal Ripken, Jr., with 8,243, from June 5, 1982 to September 14, 1987*

TODAY'S THOUGHT:

"I never had a bad night in my life, but I've had a few bad mornings." —*Lefty Gomez*

HISTORY:

On this date in 1970 Baltimore Orioles outfielder Don Buford crushed two grand slams, one from each side of the plate. He hit only 15 more home runs the rest of that season.

BIRTHDAYS:

Jose Guzman, 1963; Graeme Lloyd, 1967

TRIVIA:

Carlos Baerga of the Cleveland Indians is the only player to hit a right-handed homer and a left-handed homer in the same inning. He did it in the seventh inning of a game against the New York Yankees on April 7, 1993.

QUIZ:

Who's the only player in major league history to have a three-home run game, three times in a season?

ANSWER: *Sammy Sosa, in 2001*

TODAY'S THOUGHT:

"I dunno. I never smoked any Astroturf." —*Tug McGraw*, asked whether he preferred grass or Astroturf

HISTORY:

On this date in 1962 the expansion Houston Colt .45's won the first regular-season game played in Texas, downing the Cubs, 11-2. The day also marked the opening of Dodger Stadium, with Los Angeles falling to the Reds, 6-3.

BIRTHDAYS:

Ross Youngs, 1897; Frank Lary, 1930; Bob Watson, 1946; Ken Griffey, 1950; Al Reyes, 1970

TRIVIA:

When the Houston Astrodome opened in 1965, it used a natural Bermuda grass playing surface. But when the stadium's roof panes were painted over to remove the glare on the field, the grass died from a lack of sunlight The solution: a new type of artificial grass, which became known as Astroturf.

QUIZ:

What baseball stadium began the tradition of the "Sausage Race?"

ANSWER: *The Milwaukee Brewers' County Stadium - The tradition continued when the Brewers moved into Miller Park in 2001.*

TODAY'S THOUGHT:

"A great catch is like watching girls go by - the last one you see is always the prettiest." —*Bob Gibson*

HISTORY:

On this date in 1980 two California Angels teammates combined to no-hit the Seattle Mariners. Mark Langston pitched seven innings before Mike Witt hurled the final two frames in the 1-0 win.

BIRTHDAYS:

Bret Saberhagen, 1964; Jason Varitek, 1972; Trot Nixon, 1974; Kelvim Escobar, 1976; Mark Teixeira, 1980

TRIVIA:

The Angels' first home was Wrigley Field - an old Pacific Coast League park in Los Angeles.

EXTRA INNING:

"Kids should practice autographing baseballs. This is a skill that's often overlooked in Little League." –*Tug McGraw*

QUIZ:

Who was the last pitcher to throw 300 innings in a season?

ANSWER: *Steve Carlton pitched 304 innings in 1980.*

TODAY'S THOUGHT:

"My favorite umpire is a dead one." —*Johnny Evers*

HISTORY:

On this date in 1912 the Chicago Cubs famous double play combination of Tinker-to-Evers-to-Chance made its final appearance together in a 3-2 loss to the Cincinnati Reds. Vic Saier would replace Frank Chance at first.

BIRTHDAYS:

Vic Willis, 1876; Addie Joss, 1880; Reb Russell, 1889; Jerry Antonelli, 1930; Paul Lo Duca, 1972

TRIVIA:

While Joe Tinker, Johnny Evers and Frank Chance are all members of the Baseball Hall of Fame, the tandem was a bit over hyped. At the height of their popularity, they turned just 56 double plays in 4 years. Johnny Evers even led the league once in errors with 44 at second base.

QUIZ:

Who played third base during the Cubs' glory years from 1906 to 1910?

ANSWER: *Harry Steinfeldt - Germany Schaefer played third when the double-play combo first began in 1902, while Ed Lennox played the hot corner in their final appearance.*

April 13

TODAY'S THOUGHT:

"I'm just like everybody else. I have two arms, two legs, and four-thousand hits." —*Pete Rose*

HISTORY:

On this date in 1984 the Montreal Expos' Pete Rose belted his 4,000th hit, joining Ty Cobb as the only men to reach that milestone. Rose's first major league hit had come 21 years earlier.

BIRTHDAYS:

Wes Chamberlain, 1966; Ricardo Rincon, 1970

TRIVIA:

New York's Polo Grounds hosted baseball, football, and even boxing - but never a polo match.

EXTRA INNING:

"They're safer and faster. And they usually get your picture in the paper."
–*Pete Rose*, on why he prefers headfirst slides

QUIZ:

Who is the first player to homer in Canada in both leagues?

ANSWER: *Richie Zisk of the Pittsburgh Pirates homered in both Montreal and Toronto.*

TODAY'S THOUGHT:

"Why buy good luggage? You only use it when you travel."
—*Yogi Berra*

HISTORY:

On this date in 1969 the first Major League Baseball game outside the United States was played. The expansion Montreal Expos won their debut in front of 29,184 fans at Jarry Park, edging the St. Louis Cardinals, 8–7.

BIRTHDAYS:

Pete Rose, 1941; Greg Myers, 1966; Greg Maddux, 1966; David Justice, 1966; Brad Ausmus, 1969; Greg Zaun, 1971; Kyle Farnsworth, 1976

TRIVIA:

In only the ninth game in the team's history, Expos hurler Bill Stoneman pitched a 7–0 no-hitter against the Phillies. Then, in 1972, Stoneman pitched his second career no-hitter against the New York Mets at home, the first ever pitched outside the United States.

QUIZ:

What US President was the first to throw an Opening Day ceremonial first pitch?

ANSWER: *William Howard Taft, on April 14, 1910 - Senators right-hander Walter Johnson caught the pitch, and then went on to one-hit the Athletics, 3-0.*

TODAY'S THOUGHT:

"I figured that someday I'd have to meet my Maker and that He'd ask me why I didn't let that boy play. I was afraid that if I told Him it was because he was black, that wouldn't be sufficient." —*Happy Chandler*, former baseball commissioner, on Jackie Robinson

HISTORY:

On this date in 1947 history was made when the Dodgers' Jackie Robinson became the first African-American to play in the big leagues. Robinson went hitless in three at-bats in a 5-3 win over the Boston Braves.

BIRTHDAYS:

Willie Davis, 1940; Jeromy Burnitz, 1969; Milton Bradley, 1978

TRIVIA:

Jackie Robinson played his rookie year at first base before switching to second base the following season.

EXTRA INNING:

"If the human body recognized agony and frustration, people would never run marathons, have babies, or play baseball." –*Carlton Fisk*

QUIZ:

Three players hit better than .400 in 1922. Who were they?

ANSWER: *Rogers Hornsby won the NL batting title with a .401 average. Ty Cobb also hit .401, but lost the AL batting title to George Sisler and his .420 batting average.*

TODAY'S THOUGHT:

"I knew it was going to be a long season when, on Opening Day during the national anthem, one of my players turns to me and says, 'Every time I hear that song, I have a bad game.'" —*Jim Leyland*

HISTORY:

On this date in 1940 Bob Feller of the Cleveland Indians threw the first and only Opening Day no-hitter in major league history. Feller's Indians defeated the Chicago White Sox, 1–0, at Comiskey Park.

BIRTHDAYS:

Dutch Leonard, 1892; Paul Waner, 1903; Bruce Bochy, 1955; Fernando Vina, 1969; Antonio Alfonseca, 1972

TRIVIA:

In 1941, Feller enlisted in the Navy, and missed four seasons during his service in World War II. However, he still managed to set the major league record for most walks in a career (1,764) before he retired, a mark Nolan Ryan would later break.

QUIZ:

Can you name the only Cleveland Indians pitcher to win the Cy Young Award?

ANSWER: *Gaylord Perry, in 1972*

TODAY'S THOUGHT:

"If a tie is like kissing your sister, losing is like kissing your grandmother with her teeth out." —*George Brett*

HISTORY:

On this date in 1976 Mike Schmidt's four consecutive home runs rallied the Phillies from an eleven-run deficit against the Cubs. His home run in the 10th inning was the margin of victory in the Phils' 18-16 win.

BIRTHDAYS:

Alexander Cartwright, 1820; Cap Anson, 1852; Marquis Grissom, 1967

TRIVIA:

A Hall of Fame third baseman, Schmidt batted only .196 in his first full season in the majors.

EXTRA INNING:

"Phillies fans would boo a wake." –*Joe Dugan*

QUIZ:

Gary Cravath of Philadelphia led the National League in home runs six times. Can you name the three other sluggers who matched, or bettered, that mark?

ANSWER: *Mel Ott, six times; Ralph Kiner, seven; and Mike Schmidt, eight*

TODAY'S THOUGHT:

"Babe Ruth wasn't born. The son of a bitch fell from a tree."
—*Joe Dugan*

HISTORY:

On this date in 1923 Babe Ruth christened the "House That Ruth Built" with a three-run home run. A crowd of 74,200 attended the first game ever played in Yankee Stadium, a 4-1 triumph over the Boston Red Sox.

BIRTHDAYS:

Sam Crawford, 1880; Jim Eisenreich, 1959; Rico Brogna, 1970; Brady Clark, 1973; Miguel Cabrera, 1983

TRIVIA:

Exactly six years later, the 1929 Yankees became the first team to regularly wear numbers on the back of their uniform. Each player's number corresponded with his spot in the batting order, which is why Babe Ruth wore the number 3.

QUIZ:

True or false? When Babe Ruth hit 54 home runs in 1920 and 60 in 1927, he alone had more homers than any other team in the American League those years.

ANSWER: *True*

TODAY'S THOUGHT:

"A lot of folks that ain't saying 'ain't', ain't eating."
—*Dizzy Dean*, on his atrocious grammar

HISTORY:

On this date in 1981 the Rochester Red Wings and Pawtucket Red Sox of the International League were tied at two when play was suspended after 32 innings. The game resumed when the two teams met again later that season and ended after 18 minutes. Pawtucket scored a run in the bottom of the 33rd to win.

BIRTHDAYS:

Frank Viola, 1960; Spike Owen, 1961; Jose Cruz Jr., 1974; Joe Mauer 1983; Zach Duke, 1983

TRIVIA:

Among the professional baseball records that still stand from that game are innings, time (8:25), strikeouts (60), at-bats (219), and pitches (882). The game featured 25 future big leaguers, including Wade Boggs and Cal Ripken, Jr.

QUIZ:

I hit 399 home runs in my 22-year career, but I never hit 30 homers in one season. Who am I?

ANSWER: *Hall of Famer Al Kaline of the Detroit Tigers*

TODAY'S THOUGHT:

"Do they leave it there during games?" —*Bill Lee,* upon first seeing the left field Green Monster at Fenway

HISTORY:

On this date in 1912 and 1939 two historic debuts for the Boston Red Sox were made. In 1912, the Sox played their first game in Fenway Park, beating New York, 7-6, in 11 innings. In 1939, Ted Williams took his first swings as a major leaguer, going 1 for 4 with two strikeouts in a 2-0 Boston loss to the Yankees.

BIRTHDAYS:

Dave Bancroft, 1891; Don Mattingly, 1961; Todd Hollandsworth, 1973

TRIVIA:

Fenway Park was due to make its debut on April 18, but there were two postponements because of rain. When it did open, the news was secondary, as the sinking of the Titanic captured the headlines in Boston newspapers.

QUIZ:

Navin Field also opened the same day as Fenway. What stadium did this later become known as?

ANSWER: *After being re-named Briggs Stadium in 1938, it became Tiger Stadium in 1961.*

TODAY'S THOUGHT:

"The DH is a tenth player. Softball is ten players, baseball is nine." —*Dwight Gooden*

HISTORY:

On this date in 1994 Eddie Murray homered from both sides of the plate in a game for the eleventh time, breaking the record set by Mickey Mantle. The home runs also vaulted the Indians' first baseman past Dave Kingman on the all-time list with 444.

BIRTHDAYS:

Joe McCarthy, 1887; Gary Peters, 1937; Jesse Orosco, 1957; Ken Caminiti, 1963

TRIVIA:

Mo Vaughn wore number 42 in honor of Jackie Robinson. Now that Major League Baseball has retired the number, he was the last man to wear it.

QUIZ:

Roger Maris set the single season home run record while playing for the New York Yankees, but he also played for three other teams in his major league career. Can you name them?

ANSWER: *Cleveland Indians, Kansas City Athletics, and St. Louis Cardinals*

TODAY'S THOUGHT:

"Blind people come to the park just to listen to him pitch."
—*Reggie Jackson*, on Tom Seaver

HISTORY:

On this date in 1970 Tom Seaver tied a major league record by striking out 19 Padres in a game. Seaver fanned the last 10 batters that he faced to set still another mark in the Mets' 2-1 win.

BIRTHDAYS:

Terry Francona, 1959; Jimmy Key, 1961; Mickey Morandini, 1966

TRIVIA:

Like father, doesn't like son? In 1968 former Dodger GM Al Campanis traded his son, Jim, to the Athletics for two minor leaguers.

EXTRA INNING:

"I'd better make it, because I can't sing or dance and they've already got a pitching coach." –*Don Sutton*, on trying to make the Dodgers at the end of his career

QUIZ:

True or false? Tom Seaver never won the Cy Young Award.

ANSWER: *False- "Tom Terrific" won the award in 1969, '73 and '75.*

TODAY'S THOUGHT:

"Baseball is the most intellectual game because most of the action goes on in your head." —*Henry Kissinger*

HISTORY:

On this date in 1964 Houston pitcher Ken Johnson became the first pitcher in baseball history to lose a nine-inning no-hitter, falling to Cincinnati, 1-0. Johnson was done in by an error that allowed the only run to score.

BIRTHDAYS:

Jim Bottomley, 1900; Warren Spahn, 1921; Rheal Cormier, 1967; Andruw Jones, 1977

TRIVIA:

In 1931 Cleveland Indians' catcher Joe Sprinz caught a baseball dropped 800 feet from a balloon. The impact created such a jolt through his body that it broke his jaw.

QUIZ:

One of today's birthday boys, Andruw Jones, broke the Atlanta Braves single-season home run record in 2005. How many dingers did he hit?

ANSWER: *Fifty-one*

TODAY'S THOUGHT:

"The best thing about baseball is that you can do something about yesterday tomorrow." —*Manny Trillo*

HISTORY:

On this date in 1901 the Chicago White Stockings defeated the visiting Cleveland Blues 8-2 at South Side Park in the first game ever played in the American League. Three other games were scheduled for this day, but they were all rained out.

BIRTHDAYS:

Bob Ewing, 1873; Bill Singer, 1944; Omar Vizquel, 1967; Todd Jones, 1968; Chipper Jones, 1972; Carlos Beltran, 1977

TRIVIA:

The losing trend the Cleveland Indians developed from the '60's to the '80's became the subject of a joke: A judge asked a child in a parental custody battle which parent he wished to live with. The child said, "Neither one, they both beat me." After the judge asked who he did want to live with, the boy answered, "The Cleveland Indians, they don't beat anybody."

QUIZ:

What major league manager earned the nickname "The Human Rain Delay" in his playing days?

ANSWER: *Mike Hargrove, because of his long, drawn out routines in the batter's box*

TODAY'S THOUGHT:

"There'll be two buses leaving the hotel for the park tomorrow. The two o'clock bus for those of you who need a little extra work. The empty bus will leave at five o'clock." —*Dave Bristol*

HISTORY:

On this date in 1976 centerfielder Rick Monday came to the rescue of the American flag during a game at Dodger Stadium. Noticing two protesters kneeling on the grass in left-center attempting to burn the flag, he raced toward them and snatched it away, to thunderous applause.

BIRTHDAY:

Jacque Jones, 1975

TRIVIA:

Eric Davis was known as "Eric the Red" when he played for the Reds.

EXTRA INNING:

"I should be hungry, but I've already had breakfast and lunch tomorrow."
–*Whitey Herzog*, on a flight back from Japan

QUIZ:

What former prison inmate led the AL in stolen bases in 1978 and 1980?

ANSWER: *Ron LeFlore, who was first scouted by Detroit while he was serving time in a maximum-security prison for armed robbery*

TODAY'S THOUGHT:

"Maybe I'm not a great man but I damn well want to break the record." —*Roger Maris*

HISTORY:

On this date in 1961 Yankees outfielder Roger Maris hit his first home run of the season in a win over the Tigers. Maris picked up the pace though, hitting 60 more to break Babe Ruth's record.

BIRTHDAYS:

Hack Wilson, 1900; Sal Maglie, 1917; Amos Otis, 1947; Brian Anderson, 1972; Geoff Blum, 1973; Joe Crede, 1978

TRIVIA:

Two years earlier to the day, Sadaharu Oh hit the first home run of his Japanese baseball career. Oh went on to hit 868 home runs, the most home runs in professional baseball history.

QUIZ:

What Tigers' pitcher gave up the first of Roger Maris' 61 homers in his historic season?

ANSWER: *Paul Foytack*

TODAY'S THOUGHT:

"You're expected to be perfect the day you start, and then improve." —*Ed Vargo*, supervisor of umpires

HISTORY:

On this date in 2006 Tampa Bay minor league prospect, Delmon Young, threw his bat at the home plate umpire after being ejected for arguing a strike three call. He would later be suspended 50 games for his actions.

BIRTHDAYS:

Rogers Hornsby, 1896; Enos Slaughter, 1916; Frank Catalanotto, 1974; Pedro Feliz, 1975; Chris Carpenter, 1975; Joey Gathright, 1981

TRIVIA:

When National League umpire Tom Gorman died in 1986, he was buried in his blue umpire's suit with a ball and strike indicator in his hand. The count on it was 3-2.

QUIZ:

What's the score of a forfeited game?

ANSWER: *9-0*

TODAY'S THOUGHT:

"The only thing worse than a Mets game is a Mets doubleheader." —*Casey Stengel*, former Mets manager

HISTORY:

On this date in 1988 the winless Baltimore Orioles set a major league record by losing their 21st straight game to start the season, 4-2, to the Minnesota Twins. They would finish the year with 54 wins.

BIRTHDAY:

Barry Larkin, 1964

TRIVIA:

In 2003, by winning five of their last six games of the year, the Detroit Tigers avoided matching the 1962 New York Mets for the most single-season losses in major league history. The Tigers finished 43-119, while the Mets were 40-120.

QUIZ:

The 1962 expansion New York Mets had two players with the same first and last names. Who were they?

ANSWER: *Bob Miller and Bob Miller.*

TODAY'S THOUGHT:

"Our fielders have to catch a lot of balls - or at least deflect them to someone who can." —*Dan Quisenberry*

HISTORY:

On this date in 1986 Roger Clemens set a new major league record for strikeouts in a nine-inning game. The Bosox right-hander whiffed 20 batters, including eight in a row, in a win over Seattle.

BIRTHDAYS:

Luis Aparicio, 1934; Rick Burleson, 1951; Tony Armas, 1978

TRIVIA:

Clemens is the only player to have been the MVP, the Cy Young Award winner, and the All-Star Game MVP in the same year, 1986.

EXTRA INNING:

"In the outfield, fly balls are my only weakness." –*Carmelo Martinez*

QUIZ:

RFK Stadium, which played home to the Washington Senators and Nationals, was formerly known by what name?

ANSWER: *DC Stadium*

TODAY'S THOUGHT:

"Today, I consider myself the luckiest man on the face of the earth." —*Lou Gehrig*, in his retirement speech, before a sellout crowd at Yankee Stadium

HISTORY:

On this date in 1939 Lou Gehrig played in his 2,130th consecutive game, the last in his career. At Gehrig's request, manager Joe McCarthy removed his name from the lineup for the next game. Amyotrophic lateral sclerosis not only brought an end to his streak but claimed his life two years later.

BIRTHDAY:

Phil Garner, 1949

TRIVIA:

Lou Gehrig's salary in 1927, as a member of the Yankees' "Murderer's Row," was $8,000.

EXTRA INNING:

"I never realized how short a month is until I started paying alimony."
–*Harry Caray*

QUIZ:

Whose consecutive games-played streak did Lou Gehrig break?

ANSWER: *In 1933, Gehrig broke Everett Scott's streak of 1,307 games.*

TODAY'S THOUGHT:

"He's not Mr. October, he's Mr. May." —*George Steinbrenner*, when asked to compare Dave Winfield with Reggie Jackson

HISTORY:

On this date in 1991 Texas right-hander Nolan Ryan threw the seventh no-hitter of his career, his sixth in the American League. The 44-year old Ryan fanned 16 as he shut down Toronto, 3-0.

BIRTHDAY:

Brandon Claussen, 1979

TRIVIA:

Despite winning 324 games and striking out 5,714 batters, Nolan Ryan never won the Cy Young Award.

EXTRA INNING:

"They say some of my stars drink whiskey, but I have found that the ones who drink milk shakes don't win any ball games." –*Casey Stengel*

QUIZ:

Who was the first pitcher to throw a no-hitter and later save 40 games in a season?

ANSWER: *Dave Righetti - Righetti pitched a no-hitter on July 4, 1983, and in 1986 he set a then major league record with 46 saves.*

TODAY'S THOUGHT:

"If I'd known I was gonna pitch a no-hitter, I would have gotten a haircut." —*Bo Belinsky*

HISTORY:

On this date in 1917 Fred Toney of the Cincinnati Reds and Hippo Vaughn of the Chicago Cubs pitched a double no-hitter for nine innings. The Reds would win 1–0 on two hits in the top of the 10th. Toney retired three Cubs in the bottom of the 10th, thus completing the fourth ten-inning no-hitter to date.

BIRTHDAY:

Eddie Collins, 1887

TRIVIA:

The Reds' game-winning RBI in the game came from football, track, and Olympic star Jim Thorpe. Thorpe played in 289 major league games for the New York Giants, Reds, and Boston Braves.

QUIZ:

Who was the first Little Leaguer to become president of the United States?

ANSWER: *George W. Bush - Dubya played catcher as a Little Leaguer in Midland, Texas, from 1955 to 1958.*

TODAY'S THOUGHT:

"A player's got to be kept hungry to become a big leaguer. That's why no boy from a rich family ever made it to the big leagues." —*Joe DiMaggio*

HISTORY:

On this date in 1980 the Rangers' Ferguson Jenkins became the fourth pitcher to win one hundred games in each league, topping Baltimore, 3-2. Jenkins had won 149 games in stints with the Phillies and Cubs.

BIRTHDAYS:

Eppa Rixey, 1891; Red Ruffing, 1905; Davey Lopes, 1946; Ryan Dempster, 1977

TRIVIA:

A 1969 poll conducted to coincide with the centennial of professional baseball voted Joe DiMaggio as the greatest living ball player.

EXTRA INNING:

"I'm a David, and I'm a star." –*Dave Parker*, on why he wears a Star of David

QUIZ:

Only two players in modern baseball history have had more than 700 at bats in a season. Name them.

ANSWER: *Willie Wilson had 705 at bats for the Royals in 1980 and Juan Samuel had 701 at bats for the Phillies in 1984.*

TODAY'S THOUGHT:

"I never called a balk in my life. I didn't understand the rule."
—*Ron Luciano*, former umpire

HISTORY:

On this date in 1963 Bob Shaw of the Milwaukee Braves set a major league record by committing five balks in a single game. In the third inning, Shaw walked the Cubs' Billy Williams and with three straight balks, allowed him to score. Shaw was ejected in the fifth inning for arguing.

BIRTHDAYS:

Jack Tobin, 1892; Joe Borowski, 1971; Miguel Cairo, 1974; Jason Michaels, 1976; Ben Grieve, 1976

TRIVIA:

Dave Stewart holds the major league record for balks in a season, with 16. He set the mark in 1988, ironically one of his best years, when he posted 21 wins and pitched a career-high 14 complete games.

QUIZ:

In 1999, what major league record was officially changed due to a newly discovered scoring error?

ANSWER: *Hack Wilson's RBI record of 190 in 1930 was increased by one, to 191.*

TODAY'S THOUGHT:

"The doctors X-rayed my head and found nothing." —*Dizzy Dean*, after being hit on the head by a ball in the 1934 World Series.

HISTORY:

On this date in 1904 Cy Young of the Boston Red Sox pitched the first perfect game of the century against the Philadelphia Phillies, thus becoming the only big leaguer to hurl no-hitters before and after 1900.

BIRTHDAYS:

Chief Bender, 1884; Charles Nagy, 1976

TRIVIA:

Wade Boggs claims to have eaten a chicken meal before every game he played. Fittingly, his book of chicken recipes was called *Fowl Tips*.

EXTRA INNING:

"God is still my amigo, but he must be someplace else. Maybe he's watching the American League." –*Joaquin Andujar*, after leading the National League in losses

QUIZ:

Cy Young has the most career victories in the major leagues, 511. Who is number two on the list?

ANSWER: *Walter Johnson, with 416*

TODAY'S THOUGHT:

"I'd be the laughingstock of baseball if I changed the best left-hander in the game to an outfielder." —*Ed Barrow*, Red Sox manager, on Babe Ruth in 1918

HISTORY:

On this date in 1915 Babe Ruth, a 20-year old pitcher for the Boston Red Sox, had three hits, including his first major league home run, off the Yankees' Jack Warhop at the Polo Grounds. Ruth, however, lost the game in the 13th inning.

BIRTHDAY:

Willie Mays, 1931; Charles Nagy, 1967

TRIVIA:

Exactly three years later, Ruth would appear for the first time at a position other than pitcher. Playing first base for the Red Sox, Ruth hit a home run - against the Yankees, at the Polo Grounds, in a 10-3 loss.

QUIZ:

True or false? Babe Ruth once led the American League in earned run average (ERA) as a pitcher.

ANSWER: *True - Ruth won the title with an ERA of 1.75 in 1916.*

TODAY'S THOUGHT:

"Playing without fundamentals is like eating without a knife."
—*Dick Williams*

HISTORY:

On this date in 2003 seventy-seven year old Wayne Terwilliger became the oldest manager in minor league history. He would lead the Fort Worth Cats to the Central Baseball League championship in 2005.

BIRTHDAYS:

Dick Williams, 1929; Conor Jackson, 1982

TRIVIA:

Ken "Hawk" Harrelson, who played pro golf in addition to big league baseball, was the first major leaguer to wear a batting glove.

EXTRA INNING:

"Closed." –*Yogi Berra*, while accepting an honorary degree from Roger Williams University, when asked how he liked school

QUIZ:

What player would have tied Babe Ruth's single-season home run record in 1932 if rainouts hadn't erased two homers?

ANSWER: *Jimmie Foxx - Foxx crushed 58 home runs in 1932, but lost two of them because of games called off before the fifth inning.*

TODAY'S THOUGHT:

"The sun don't shine on the same dog's ass all the time."
—*Catfish Hunter*

HISTORY:

On this date in 1968 Jim "Catfish" Hunter pitched the American League's first perfect game in 46 years as the A's beat the Twins, 4-0. At age 22, Hunter became the youngest player ever to do it.

BIRTHDAYS:

Dan Brouthers, 1858; Edd Roush, 1893; Mike Cuellar, 1937; Adrian Gonzalez, 1982

TRIVIA:

In the game, Hunter was almost as impressive at the plate. He got three hits and drove in all four of the A's runs. He would finish the season with eight RBIs.

QUIZ:

Who holds the record among pitchers (who don't play other positions) for the most home runs hit in a single season?

ANSWER: *Wes Ferrell, who hit 9 homers in 1931*

TODAY'S THOUGHT:

"I'm happy I played 20 years - I played them all here in San Diego. So the back of my bubblegum card from here to eternity will look pretty good." —*Tony Gwynn*

HISTORY:

On this date in 1961 Baltimore Orioles first baseman Jim Gentile set a major league record, hitting grand slam homers in consecutive at bats. Gentile led the American League that year with 141 RBIs.

BIRTHDAYS:

Tony Gwynn,1960; Brandon Webb, 1979; Prince Fielder, 1984

TRIVIA:

Al Oliver was the first big league player to wear the number 0. The Rangers' outfielder, however, insisted it was an "O" for Oliver, not a zero.

EXTRA INNING:

"I was such a dangerous hitter; I even got intentional walks in batting practice." –*Casey Stengel*, on his playing days

QUIZ:

Who was the only player ever to be traded after winning the Triple Crown?

ANSWER: *Chuck Klein won the Triple Crown in 1933 with the Phillies and was traded to the Cubs after the season.*

TODAY'S THOUGHT:

"There are two ways to catch a knuckleball. Unfortunately, neither of them works." —*Hitting instructor Charlie Lau*

HISTORY:

On this date in 1970 Braves' knuckleballer Hoyt Wilhelm became the first major league pitcher to appear in 1,000 games. He made a relief appearance against the St. Louis Cardinals, giving up three runs, as Atlanta lost, 6-5.

BIRTHDAY:

Ed Barrow, 1868

TRIVIA:

In 1985, Wilhelm became the first reliever elected to the Hall of Fame. He also is one of only two players in the Hall (Earl Averill is the other) to hit a home run in his first major league at bat. It was the only one he would ever hit.

QUIZ:

What major league pitcher holds the single-season save record?

ANSWER: *Bobby Thigpen, who saved 57 games for the Chicago White Sox in 1990*

TODAY'S THOUGHT:

"He hits .350 on opening day and stays there all season."
—*Lefty Gomez* on Charlie Gehringer

HISTORY:

On this date in 1963 Sandy Koufax no-hit the San Francisco Giants, 8-0. It marked the second consecutive season that the Dodger southpaw had hurled a no-hitter.

BIRTHDAYS:

Charlie Gehringer, 1903; Rip Sewell, 1907; Francisco Cordero, 1975

TRIVIA:

Charlie Gehringer played every inning of the first six All-Star Games as the starting second baseman for the American League. He batted .500 in 20 All-Star at-bats.

EXTRA INNING:

"It's permanent, for now." –Cincinnati Red *Roberto Kelly*, announcing his new name would be Bobby

QUIZ:

Who played the most games for the Montreal Expos?

ANSWER: *Tim Wallach - Wallach played in 1,767 games for the Expos from 1980-1992.*

TODAY'S THOUGHT:

"Good pitching always stops good hitting and vice versa."
—*Bob Veale*

HISTORY:

On this date in 1955 Sam "Toothpick" Jones became the first black pitcher to throw a no-hitter in major league history, as his Cubs beat the Pirates, 4-0. But it wasn't easy. After walking the bases loaded in the ninth, Jones struck out Dick Groat, Roberto Clemente, and Frank Thomas to close it out.

BIRTHDAYS:

Yogi Berra, 1925; Felipe Alou, 1935; Lou Whitaker, 1957; Wes Helms, 1976; Josh Phelps, 1978; Felipe Lopez, 1980

TRIVIA:

The Cubs' Sam Jones actually became the second player named Sam Jones to throw a no-hitter. The first Sam pitched for 22 years in the AL, and no-hit Philadelphia in 1923 while pitching for the Yankees.

QUIZ:

Who is the only major league pitcher to have thrown no-hitters in four consecutive seasons?

ANSWER: *Sandy Koufax, from 1962 to 1965*

TODAY'S THOUGHT:

"Other sports are just sports, baseball is a love."
—*Bryant Gumbel*

HISTORY:

On this date in 1958 Stan Musial of the St. Louis Cardinals recorded his 3,000th hit, a pinch-hit double off Cubs pitcher Moe Drabowsky. Stan the Man ended his 22-year career with 3,630 hits and a batting average of .331.

BIRTHDAYS:

Bobby Valentine, 1950; Jose Rijo, 1965; Barry Zito, 1978

TRIVIA:

Stan Musial was the first inductee into the Polish-American Sports Hall of Fame and Museum.

EXTRA INNING:

"Everybody got married in the off-season. We might have the best road record in baseball this season." –Newlywed Boston Red Sox reliever *Wes Gardner*

QUIZ:

"The Mad Hungarian", "The Mahatma", and "The Grey Eagle" were the nicknames of what baseball figures?

ANSWER: *Al Hrabosky, Branch Rickey and Tris Speaker.*

May 14

TODAY'S THOUGHT:

"It isn't hard to be good from time to time in sports. What's tough is being good every day." —*Willie Mays*

HISTORY:

On this date in 1972 Willie Mays, acquired by the Mets for a player and cash, made his return to New York at the age of 41. Mays hit a fifth-inning homer that proved to be the difference in the 5-4 win over his former club, the Giants.

BIRTHDAYS:

Ed Walsh, 1881; Earle Combs, 1899; Tony Perez, 1942; Dennis Martinez, 1955; Brian Lawrence, 1976; Roy Halladay, 1977

TRIVIA:

Willie Mays was the on-deck batter when Bobby Thomson hit his famous pennant-winning home run, "The Shot Heard 'Round the World," in 1951.

QUIZ:

True or false? Richie Ashburn won more National League batting titles than Willie Mays.

ANSWER: *True - Ashburn was the NL batting champ in 1955 and '58. Mays won the title once in 1954.*

May 15

TODAY'S THOUGHT:

"George Brett could roll out of bed on Christmas morning and hit a line drive." —*John Schuerholtz*, Royals GM

HISTORY:

On this date in 1981 Len Barker threw the tenth perfect game in major league history on a cold and rainy night in Cleveland. Less than 8,000 fans saw Barker strike out 11 in a 3-0 win over Toronto.

BIRTHDAYS:

George Brett, 1953; John Smoltz, 1967; Hideki Irabu, 1969; Josh Beckett, 1980; Justin Morneau, 1981

TRIVIA:

The uniform number "10" has been retired by the Expos (Rusty Staub), Royals (Dick Howser), Yankees (Phil Rizzuto), and Cubs (Ron Santo).

EXTRA INNING:

"If you hit [Luis] Polonia 100 fly balls, you could make a movie out of it – *Catch-22*." –*Dennis Lamp*

QUIZ:

I'm the Cleveland third baseman who made two great plays to help stop Joe DiMaggio's 56-game hitting streak in 1941. Who am I?

ANSWER: *Ken Keltner*

TODAY'S THOUGHT:

"Mathewson pitched against Cincinnati yesterday. Another way of putting it is that Cincinnati lost a game of baseball. The first statement means the same as the second." —*Writer Damon Runyon*

HISTORY:

On this date in 1913 Christy Mathewson's string of perfect control for 47 innings was broken when he walked the Pirates' Ed Mensor in the third inning. Mensor drew just eight walks the entire year. Mathewson lost the streak but gained the win, 7–4, for the Giants.

BIRTHDAYS:

Billy Martin, 1928; Rick Reuschel, 1949; Jack Morris, 1955; Doug Brocail, 1967; Jim Mecir, 1970

TRIVIA:

Mathewson was extremely intellegent, and was an accomplished checkers player. In fact, he once defeated the world checkers champion, Newell Banks.

QUIZ:

What pitcher is the only athlete to have played on championship teams in both Major League Baseball and the NBA?

ANSWER: *Gene Conley, who played on the 1957 World Series champion Milwaukee Braves and the NBA champion Boston Celtics from 1959-61*

TODAY'S THOUGHT:

"Any time you think you have the game conquered, the game will turn around and punch you right in the nose."
—*Mike Schmidt*

HISTORY:

On this date in 1979 Mike Schmidt's second homer of the game in the 10th inning gave the Phillies a 23-22 win over the Cubs. The wind was blowing out that day at Wrigley Field as the two teams combined to hit 11 home runs, including three by the Cubs' Dave Kingman.

BIRTHDAYS:

James "Cool Papa" Bell, 1903; Jose Guillen, 1976; Carlos Pena, 1978

TRIVIA:

A statue of Mike Schmidt honors the Hall of Famer outside the third base gate at Citizens Bank Park in Philadelphia.

EXTRA INNING:

"I've seen better hands on a clock." – Sportswriter *Mel Durslag*, after Bill Russell made five errors in a doubleheader

QUIZ:

What baseball franchise has fielded a team for the most years without a World Series appearance?

ANSWER: *The Texas Rangers, since 1961 when they were the expansion Washington Senators - They moved to Texas in 1972.*

TODAY'S THOUGHT:

"I was a victim of circumcision." —*Pete Vukovich*, Pirates pitching coach, after being ejected from a game for arguing

HISTORY:

On this date in 1912 Detroit Tigers' players went on strike to protest Ty Cobb's suspension for attacking a fan in New York. Playing against Philadelphia with a team made up of amateurs and coaches, the Tigers were mauled by the Athletics, 24-2.

BIRTHDAYS:

Babe Adams, 1882; Brooks Robinson, 1937; Reggie Jackson, 1946; Eric Young, 1967; Marcus Giles, 1978

TRIVIA:

Former college pitcher Alousius Travers made the start for the short-handed Tigers. In his eight innings of work he yielded 26 hits, 7 walks, and allowed all 24 Philadelphia runs. For their efforts, the Tigers' replacements received $50 apiece.

QUIZ:

How wide is home plate?

ANSWER: *Seventeen inches*

TODAY'S THOUGHT:

"When a pitcher's throwing a spit ball, don't worry and don't complain, just hit the dry side like I do." —*Stan Musial*

HISTORY:

On this date in 1960 Juan Marichal made his pitching debut for the San Francisco Giants. It was an impressive one, too, as the "Dominican Dandy" shut out the Phillies, 1-0, on one hit.

BIRTHDAYS:

Curt Simmons, 1929; Turk Wendell, 1967; Brandon Inge, 1977

TRIVIA:

Hall of Famer Stan Musial tallied 475 home runs in his career, but never hit 40 in a season.

EXTRA INNING:

"It's the first time in my career I was booed coming into a game. Usually they boo after I leave." –Relief pitcher *Bob Stanley*

QUIZ:

Who was the first New York Met to homer at Yankee Stadium in a regular-season game: a) John Olerud b) Edgardo Alfonzo c) Bernard Gilkey; d) Mike Piazza?

ANSWER: *c) Bernard Gilkey homered off David Wells in 1998 in the second regular season game ever played between the teams.*

TODAY'S THOUGHT:

"I wanted to be like Nolan Ryan. I didn't want to be like Pete Gray."
—*Jim Abbott*

HISTORY:

On this date in 1945 lead-off hitter Pete Gray drove in two runs with three hits as the St. Louis Browns beat the Yankees, 10-1. Gray was a leftfielder…a one-armed leftfielder.

BIRTHDAYS:

Joe Harris, 1891; George Grantham, 1900; Hal Newhouser, 1921; Ken Boyer, 1931; Bobby Murcer, 1946; David Wells, 1963; Todd Stottlemyre, 1965; Ramon Hernandez, 1976; Austin Kearns, 1980

TRIVIA:

Gray, who lost his right arm in a childhood accident, gained national attention with the semi-pro Memphis Chicks when he batted .333 and stole a record 68 bases in 1944. That year, he was named the Southern Association's MVP.

QUIZ:

Who was the first Angels' pitcher of the new millennium to win 20 games in a season?

ANSWER: *Bartolo Colon, who went 21-8 in 2005*

TODAY'S THOUGHT:

"You spend a good piece of your life gripping a baseball and in the end it turns out that it was the other way around all the time." —*Jim Bouton*

HISTORY:

On this date in 1952 the Brooklyn Dodgers scored a major league-record 15 first-inning runs against the Cincinnati Reds. After the first batter was retired, the next 19 Dodgers reached base en route to a 19-1 victory.

BIRTHDAYS:

Earl Averill, 1902; Bobby Cox, 1941; Kent Hrbek, 1960

TRIVIA:

Birthday boy Bobby Cox is by almost all accounts one of the best managers in baseball history. Don't tell that to the umpires, though. Cox has been known for his short temper with them and, in fact, is the only person - player or manager – to have been ejected from two World Series games (once in 1992, and again in 1996).

QUIZ:

Fear Strikes Out was a movie based on the life of major league outfielder Jimmy Piersall. What actor starred as Piersall?

ANSWER: *Anthony Perkins*

TODAY'S THOUGHT:

"If I had played my career hitting singles like Pete, I'd wear a dress." —*Mickey Mantle*, on Pete Rose

HISTORY:

On this date in 1963 Mickey Mantle, using a borrowed bat from Dale Long, crushed a solo home run off A's pitcher Bill Fischer to win the game for the Yankees in the eleventh inning, 8-7. The shot, which would have traveled an estimated 620 feet, was still rising when it struck the facade 100 feet above the field at Yankee Stadium.

BIRTHDAYS:

Al Simmons, 1902; Tommy John, 1943; Jose Mesa, 1966; Julian Tavarez, 1973; Chad Tracy, 1980

TRIVIA:

Until 1857, when baseball adopted the nine innings per game rule, the first team to score 21 runs was declared the winner.

QUIZ:

Who holds the American League record for the most RBIs in a season?

ANSWER: *Lou Gehrig, with 184 in 1931*

TODAY'S THOUGHT:

"Why does everyone stand up and sing *Take Me Out to the Ballgame* when they're already there?" —*Larry Anderson*

HISTORY:

On this date in 2002 Los Angeles Dodgers' outfielder Shawn Green hit four home runs in a 16-3 rout of the Atlanta Braves. Green went 6 for 6 in the game, scored seven runs, had seven RBIs and a major league record 19 total bases.

BIRTHDAYS:

Zack Wheat, 1888; Buck Showalter, 1956

TRIVIA:

Shawn Green holds the Dodgers record for most home runs in a season, 49 in 2001.

EXTRA INNING:

"The manager used to have a bed check for me every night. No problem; my bed was always there." –*Bob Veale*

QUIZ:

Who won three Cy Young Awards unanimously?

ANSWER: *Sandy Koufax, in 1963, 1965 and 1966*

TODAY'S THOUGHT:

"He sat right where I usually sit. I didn't have the heart to say, 'Move over.'" —*Joe Altobelli*, on President Ronald Reagan sitting in Altobelli's seat in the dugout on Opening Day

HISTORY:

On this date in 1935 President Franklin Delano Roosevelt pressed a button at the White House that turned the lights on at Cincinnati's Crosley Field for Major League Baseball's first night game. The Reds beat the Phillies on this historic night, 2-1.

BIRTHDAYS:

Bartolo Colon, 1973; Jae Seo, 1977; Brad Penny, 1978; Joe Kennedy, 1979

TRIVIA:

Former president Ronald Reagan once worked as a radio announcer for the Chicago Cubs in the 1930's. His success gave him the opportunity to pursue acting, where he once played Grover Cleveland, a pitching prospect, in *The Winning Team*.

QUIZ:

What former US president played in the first ever College World Series?

ANSWER: *George H. W. Bush - He was the captain of Yale's college baseball team that lost in the 1947 College World Series to California.*

TODAY'S THOUGHT:

"If I'd just tried for some dinky singles I could've batted around .600." —*Babe Ruth*

HISTORY:

On this date in 1935 Babe Ruth hit three home runs and drove in six runs as his Boston Braves lost to the Pittsburgh Pirates 11-7. Ruth's third homer, which cleared the right field grandstand at Forbes Field, was the final one of his career.

BIRTHDAYS:

Dave Hollins, 1966; Todd Walker, 1973; Miguel Tejada, 1976

TRIVIA:

During World War II, American GI's reported that Japanese soldiers would shout at them "To hell with Babe Ruth!"

EXTRA INNING:

"Home-run hitters drive Cadillacs; singles hitters drive Fords." –*Ralph Kiner*

QUIZ:

Who is the first American Leaguer in the 20th century, other than Babe Ruth, to hit 30 home runs in a season?

ANSWER: *Ken Williams, who hit 39 homers for the St. Louis Browns in 1922*

TODAY'S THOUGHT:

"I probably got more famous from losing the perfect game in thirteen innings than if I had won it in nine!" —*Harvey Haddix*

HISTORY:

On this date in 1959 Pittsburgh pitcher Harvey Haddix was perfect for 12 innings, but an error, an intentional walk of Hank Aaron, and a double by Joe Adcock allowed the Braves to get by the Pirates and Haddix, 1-0, in 13 innings.

BIRTHDAYS:

Darrell Evans, 1947; Kevin Kennedy, 1954; Travis Lee, 1975

TRIVIA:

The Pirates adopted the popular Sister Sledge disco anthem *We Are Family* as their theme song during their fifth World Series Championship run in 1979. They fought back from a 3-1 series deficit against the Orioles to take the title in Game 7.

QUIZ:

Only 18 balls were hit out of Pittsburgh's Forbes Field in the park's 61-year history. Name the player who hit seven of them.

ANSWER: *Willie Stargell*

TODAY'S THOUGHT:

"A fellow doesn't last long on what he has done. He has to keep on delivering." —*Carl Hubbell*

HISTORY:

On this date in 1937 New York Giants pitcher Carl Hubbell defeated the Cincinnati Reds, 3-2, which gave him his 24th consecutive victory over two seasons. The man known as "King Carl" won a total of 48 games in the 1936 and '37 seasons.

BIRTHDAYS:

Frank Thomas, 1968; Jeff Bagwell, 1968; Todd Hundley, 1969

TRIVIA:

Al Benton was the only pitcher to face Babe Ruth and Mickey Mantle in a major league game - Ruth in 1934 and Mantle in 1952.

QUIZ:

What stadium had the largest seating capacity for any Major League Baseball team?

ANSWER: *The Memorial Coliseum in Los Angeles, where the Dodgers played from 1958-1961, had a capacity of 93,600.*

TODAY'S THOUGHT:

"I wanted to go into my home run trot, but I realized I didn't have one." —*Jim Essian*, after hitting his first home run in more than 100 games

HISTORY:

On this date in 1956 Pirates first baseman Dale Long became the first player to homer in eight staight games, when he connected off Brooklyn's Carl Erskine in a Pittsburgh victory over the Dodgers.

BIRTHDAYS:

Kirk Gibson, 1957; Daniel Cabrera, 1981; Jhonny Peralta, 1982

TRIVIA:

Long was not known as a prolific home run hitter. He hit 27 homers in 1956, which was by far his best single-season total as a pro. In his 10-year big league career, he produced only 132 total home runs.

QUIZ:

Two other major leaguers besides Dale Long have homered in eight consecutive games. Who are they?

ANSWER: *Don Mattingly and Ken Griffey, Jr.*

TODAY'S THOUGHT:

"Never trust a base runner who's limping. Come a base hit and you'll think he just got back from Lourdes." *—Joe Garagiola*

HISTORY:

On this date in 1990 Rickey Henderson of the Oakland A's passed Ty Cobb as the American League's all-time stolen base leader, swiping number 893 in a 2-1 loss to Toronto.

BIRTHDAYS:

Fay Vincent, 1938; Eric Davis, 1962

TRIVIA:

Henderson had four different stints with the Oakland A's. He played for the team from 1979-84, '89-'93, '94-'95, and 1998.

EXTRA INNING:

"My ultimate dream is to have my own bank, maybe in Paris. I'd call it, 'Banks' Bank on the Left Bank.'" *–Ernie Banks*

QUIZ:

Excluding Colorado, Florida, and Tampa Bay, which is the only major league franchise that has not had a Cy Young Award winner?

ANSWER: *The Cincinnati Reds*

TODAY'S THOUGHT:

"Winfield goes back to the wall. He hits his head on the wall and it rolls off! It's rolling all the way back to second base! This is a terrible thing for the Padres!"

—*Jerry Coleman,* Padres radio announcer

HISTORY:

On this date in 1904 Cubs first baseman Frank Chance was hit by a pitch a record five times in a doubleheader in Cincinnati. In the first game, he was hit in the head and knocked unconscious, but came to and kept on playing.

BIRTHDAYS:

Amos Rusie, 1871; Mike Donlin, 1878; Manny Ramirez, 1972; Scott Eyre, 1972

TRIVIA:

Chance's encounter marked the second time in three years he'd been hit three times in a game. Beanings over his 17-year career severely damaged his vision and might have contributed to his death at age 47.

QUIZ:

The famous Tinker-to-Evers-to-Chance double play combo was remembered in what poem written by newspaper columnist Franklin Pierce Adams?

ANSWER: *Baseball's Sad Lexicon*

TODAY'S THOUGHT:

"I tell it like it is. Howard Cosell tells it like Roone Arledge wants it told." —*Harry Caray*

HISTORY:

On this date in 1927 Detroit Tigers first baseman Johnny Neun recorded an unassisted triple play. Amazingly, this occurred one day after Jimmy Cooney pulled one off for the Chicago Cubs.

BIRTHDAYS:

Joe Orsulak, 1962; Kenny Lofton, 1967; Dave Roberts, 1972; Jake Peavy, 1981

TRIVIA:

Charlie Brown's favorite baseball player in the *Peanuts* comic strip is Joe Shlabotnik.

EXTRA INNING:

"You have a left and a right. The left side controls the right half of your body, and the right side controls the left half. Therefore, left-handers are the only people in their right mind." –*Bill Lee*, former Red Sox pitcher, on brain hemispheres

QUIZ:

It *Pays to Steal* was the 1963 autobiography of what speedster?

ANSWER: *Maury Wills, who pilfered 104 bases that year*

TODAY'S THOUGHT:

"Baseball is the only endeavor where a man can succeed three times out of ten and be considered a good performer."
—*Ted Williams*

HISTORY:

On this date in 1987 Phil Niekro earned his 314th career victory as his Indians beat the Tigers. The win gave him and his brother, Joe, a major league record 530 combined wins, surpassing the mark set by the Perry brothers, Gaylord and Jim.

BIRTHDAYS:

Dean Chance, 1941; Derek Lowe, 1973; Brad Wilkerson, 1977; Carlos Zambrano, 1981

TRIVIA:

In 1908 Hall of Fame pitcher Walter Johnson pitched three shutouts in four days, allowing a grand total of twelve hits.

QUIZ:

Name the only player in major league history to play all 162 games for his team in the field and not commit an error:

a) Rocky Colavito
b) Darren Lewis
c) Gary Pettis
d) Ryne Sandberg

ANSWER: *a) Rocky Colavito of the Cleveland Indians*

TODAY'S THOUGHT:

"Like they say, it ain't over till the fat guy swings." —*Phillies catcher Darren Daulton*, on stocky first baseman John Kruk

HISTORY:

On this date in 1935 the playing career of Babe Ruth came to an end. Boston Braves' owner Emil Fuchs gave the 41-year old slugger his unconditional release.

BIRTHDAYS:

Jim Maloney, 1940; Mike Stanton, 1967; Raul Ibanez, 1972; Neifi Perez, 1973

TRIVIA:

Exactly six years later another Yankee legacy would come to an end, but in a more tragic way. Thirty-seven year old Lou Gehrig died at his home from amyotrophic lateral sclerosis, a disease that would later be named after him.

EXTRA INNING:

"Sorry, but I still can't figure out the right joke about Jeff Kent hitting for the cycle." –*Steve Rosenbloom* of the *Chicago Tribune*, after Kent was injured following a motorbike accident

QUIZ:

"The outlook wasn't brilliant..." begins what famous poem?

ANSWER: *Ernest Lawrence Thayer's Casey at the Bat*

TODAY'S THOUGHT:

"I believe in the Rip Van Winkle theory: That a man from 1910 must be able to wake up after being asleep for seventy years, walk into a ballpark and understand baseball perfectly." —*Bowie Kuhn*

HISTORY:

On this date in 1932 Lou Gehrig became the first major leaguer to hit four consecutive home runs in a game as the Yankees defeated the A's, 20-13, in a slugfest.

BIRTHDAYS:

Carl Everett, 1971; Travis Hafner, 1977; Juan Rivera, 1978

TRIVIA:

The New York Knickerbockers became the first pro baseball club to wear hats - straw hats - in 1852.

EXTRA INNING:

"Both have been real nice." –*Bob Brenly*, on the fans' acceptance of the Giants despite a bad season

QUIZ:

What player with over 3,000 hits had exactly the same amount of hits at home as on the road?

ANSWER: *Stan Musial, with 1,815*

TODAY'S THOUGHT:

"Statistics are used by baseball fans in much the same way that a drunk leans against a street lamp; it's there more for support than enlightenment." —*Vin Scully*

HISTORY:

On this date in 1968 the Dodgers' Don Drysdale pitched a record sixth straight shutout, defeating the Pittsburgh Pirates 5–0. He set another record for the most consecutive scoreless innings pitched, with 54. His streak would come to an end at 58.

BIRTHDAYS:

John McNamara, 1932; Tony Pena, 1957; Darin Erstad, 1974; J.C Romero, 1976

TRIVIA:

Drysdale's record would stand for 20 years until another Dodger, Orel Hershiser, threw 59 straight shutout innings, a record that still stands. In that 1988 season, Hershiser led the league in wins (23), innings pitched (267), and complete games (15).

QUIZ:

In 1986, Don Drysdale married what female member of the Basketball Hall of Fame?

ANSWER: *Ann Meyers - It was the first time that a married couple were members of their respective sports' Halls of Fame.*

TODAY'S THOUGHT:

"A hot dog at the ballpark is better than steak at the Ritz."
—*Humphrey Bogart*

HISTORY:

On this date in 1989 Toronto's SkyDome, the new home of the Blue Jays, opened. With its retractable roof, it was considered to be the most advanced ballpark for its time. Toronto lost to the Brewers, 5-3, in the inaugural game.

BIRTHDAYS:

Jack Chesbro, 1874; Ray Lankford, 1967; Russ Ortiz, 1974

TRIVIA:

In 1952 Bristol, Virginia pitcher Ron Necciai struck out 27 batters in a nine-inning Appalachian League game against Welch, West Virginia.

QUIZ:

Who was the only pitcher to win three consecutive Triple Crowns - wins, strikeouts, and ERA - in the 20th century?

ANSWER: *Grover Cleveland Alexander, who won Triple Crowns from 1915-17 pitching for the Philadelphia Phillies*

TODAY'S THOUGHT:

"I love the fact that I can go up to the plate and do things right more than anybody else." —*Tony Gwynn*

HISTORY:

On this date in 1992 Eddie Murray passed Mickey Mantle to become baseball's all-time RBI leader among switch-hitters. With two runs batted in, he ran his RBI total to 1,510 in a 15-1 Mets' win over the Pirates.

BIRTHDAYS:

Bill Dickey, 1907; Tony Graffanino, 1972; Mark Ellis, 1977; Jeremy Affeldt, 1979

TRIVIA:

Murray attended Locke High School in Los Angeles, California, where he batted .500 as a senior. Murray was a teammate of fellow Hall of Famer, St. Louis Cardinals' legend Ozzie Smith.

EXTRA INNING:

"They should move back first base a step to eliminate all the close plays."
–*John Lowenstein*

QUIZ:

On June 6, 1892, what president became the first to attend a Major League Baseball game?

ANSWER: *Benjamin Harrison*

TODAY'S THOUGHT:

"You have to have a catcher or you'll have all passed balls."
—*Casey Stengel*

HISTORY:

On this date in 1966 St. Louis Cardinals pitcher Bob Gibson tied a major league record when he struck out 4 batters in one inning, but was pulled in the seventh inning of a 9-1 loss to Pittsburgh.

BIRTHDAYS:

Thurman Munson, 1947; Odalis Perez, 1977

TRIVIA:

Bob Gibson is the last National League pitcher to win the Most Valuable Player Award (1968).

EXTRA INNING:

"I refuse to call a 47-year-old white-haired man Sparky." –*Al Clarke*, umpire, on Sparky Anderson

QUIZ:

In 1913, he became the first pitcher to win the MVP Award. Name him.

ANSWER: *The Senators' Walter Johnson*

TODAY'S THOUGHT:

"The rhythms of the game are so similar to the pattern of American life. Periods of leisure, interrupted by bursts of frantic activity." —*Roger Kahn*, on baseball

HISTORY:

On this date in 1961 the Milwaukee Braves set a major league record with four consecutive home runs in the seventh inning against the Reds. Eddie Mathews, Hank Aaron, Joe Adcock, and Frank Thomas hit the back-to-back-to-back-to-back homers.

BIRTHDAYS:

Del Ennis, 1925; Mark Belanger, 1944; Dave Mlicki, 1968

TRIVIA:

For the '61 season, Adcock finished fifth in the league in homers with 35, Aaron sixth with 34, and Mathews seventh with 32. Thomas had "only" 25. When the four teammates ended their major league careers, they combined for a total of 1,889 homers.

QUIZ:

Who is the National League career leader in grand slams?

ANSWER: *Willie McCovey, with 18*

TODAY'S THOUGHT:

"I didn't have evil intentions, but I guess I did have power."
—*Harmon Killebrew*

HISTORY:

On this date in 1966 the Minnesota Twins hit five home runs in one inning. Rich Rollins, Zoilo Versalles, Tony Oliva, Don Mincher and Harmon Killebrew each connected in the seventh inning to help the Twins defeat the Royals, 9-4.

BIRTHDAYS:

Bill Virdon, 1931; Dave Parker, 1951; Randy Winn, 1974

TRIVIA:

The first designated hitter to homer was the Twins' Tony Oliva.

EXTRA INNING:

"The other day I watched the Rockies taking batting practice and the pitching machine threw a no-hitter." –Colorado Rockies radio announcer *Pete Jones*

QUIZ:

The spitball was officially banned in 1920, but seventeen pitchers were allowed to continue to use it in the major leagues. Who threw the last "legal" spitter?

ANSWER: *Burleigh Grimes, in 1934*

TODAY'S THOUGHT:

"I'll tell you how smart Pete is. When they had the blackout in New York, he was stranded 13 hours on an escalator."
—*Joe Nuxhall,* on Pete Rose

HISTORY:

On this date in 1944 Joe Nuxhall, at 15 years, 10 months and 11 days, became the youngest player in major league history when he pitched 2/3 of an inning for the Cincinnati Reds. Nuxhall gave up five runs in an 18–0 loss to the St. Louis Cardinals.

BIRTHDAYS:

Frank Demaree, 1910; Ken Singleton, 1947; Pokey Reese, 1973; Freddy Garcia, 1976

TRIVIA:

Nuxhall's hideous 67.50 ERA from that game stayed with him until eight years later, when he made his second appearance. He would spend 15 more years in the majors, winning 135 games. His career ERA - 3.90.

QUIZ:

In 1968, what pitcher finished the season with a major league record low ERA of 1.12?

ANSWER: *Bob Gibson*

TODAY'S THOUGHT:

"Ronald Reagan has held the two most demeaning jobs in the country - President of the United States and radio broadcaster of the Chicago Cubs." —*George Will*

HISTORY:

On this date in 1985 Phillies outfielder Von Hayes became the first major leaguer to hit two home runs in the first inning. His leadoff homer and grand slam propelled Philadelphia to a 26-7 victory over the Mets.

BIRTHDAY:

Jose Reyes, 1983

TRIVIA:

The longest home run hit at Wrigley Field was 550 feet by Dave Kingman. Kingman hit a shot that landed on the third porch roof on the east (center field) side of Kenmore Avenue.

EXTRA INNING:

"I've reserved three seats for you at my show tonight. One for you, one for your wife, and one for your stomach." –Comedian *Don Rickles*, to former major-league skipper Don Zimmer

QUIZ:

Who played in each of the New York Mets' first 18 years of existence?

ANSWER: *"Steady Eddie" Kranepool*

June 12

TODAY'S THOUGHT:

"Saying that men talk about baseball in order to avoid talking about their feelings is the same as saying that women talk about their feelings in order to avoid talking about baseball." —*Deborah Tannen*

HISTORY:

On this date in 1939 the National Baseball Hall of Fame and Museum officially opened its doors in Cooperstown, NY. Ceremonies were officiated by Commissioner Kenesaw Mountain Landis and featured the official induction of its first 26 members, spanning the classes of 1936 to '39.

BIRTHDAYS:

Ryan Klesko, 1971; Hideki Matsui, 1974

TRIVIA:

Abbott and Costello are the only two members of the Baseball Hall of Fame not affiliated with baseball. This comedy team was honored for its zany *Who's on First?* routine.

QUIZ:

True or false? Cooperstown, New York, the home of the Baseball Hall of Fame, was named for the father of novelist James Fenimore Cooper.

ANSWER: *True*

TODAY'S THOUGHT:

"My only day off is the day I pitch." —*Roger Clemens*

HISTORY:

On this date in 2003 Roger Clemens of the New York Yankees recorded his 300th win, 5-2, over the St. Louis Cardinals. Clemens also became the third pitcher in history to record 4,000 career strikeouts.

BIRTHDAY:

Mel Parnell, 1922

TRIVIA:

The quickest Major League Baseball game was a 6-1 Giants win over the Phillies in 1919 - just 51 minutes!

EXTRA INNING:

"I've been called everything but my name." –*Dave Phillips*, umpire

QUIZ:

Ted Danson played what fictional retired pitcher for the Boston Red Sox in the hit television series *Cheers*?

ANSWER: *Sam Malone*

TODAY'S THOUGHT:

"Always root for the winner. That way you won't be disappointed." —*Tug McGraw*

HISTORY:

On this date in 1870 the Cincinnati Red Stockings, baseball's first all-professional team, finally lost a game, an extra inning defeat to the Atlantics of Brooklyn. The Red Stockings had won 130 games in a row between 1869 & 1870.

BIRTHDAY:

Don Newcombe, 1926

TRIVIA:

The longest winning streak in the history of Major League Baseball is 26, set back in 1916 by the New York Giants. That team, however, finished in fourth place in the NL, with a record of 86-66.

EXTRA INNING:

"We have a good bench. The trouble is, they're starting." –An Anonymous Chicago Cub

QUIZ:

Who is the winningest manager in major league history?

ANSWER: *Connie Mack, who won 3,731 regular season games (He also lost 3,948, another record.)*

TODAY'S THOUGHT:

"Greg Maddux is the prime example of a fast worker…Maddux is the type of guy who would've told Lincoln to hurry up his *Gettysburg Address* or told Chopin to shorten his *Minute Waltz.*" —*Tim McCarver*

HISTORY:

On this date in 1938 Cincinnati's Johnny Vander Meer became the only pitcher in baseball history to throw two consecutive no-hitters. Vander Meer shut out the Dodgers, 6-0, four days after not allowing a hit to the Boston Braves.

BIRTHDAYS:

Billy Williams, 1938; Dusty Baker, 1949; Brett Butler, 1957; Wade Boggs, 1958; Ramiro Mendoza, 1972; Andy Pettitte, 1972; Tony Clark, 1972

TRIVIA:

Vander Meer's nickname was "Dutch Master," but he also became known as "Double No-Hit" after his historic accomplishment.

QUIZ:

Playing by the rules: A runner standing on third base is hit by a line drive. Is he safe or out?

ANSWER: *Out*

TODAY'S THOUGHT:

"In 1962, I was voted Minor League Player of the Year. Unfortunately, that was my second year in the majors."
—*Bob Uecker*

HISTORY:

On this date in 1909 multi-sport star Jim Thorpe made his baseball pitching debut for Rocky Mount of the Eastern Carolina League, earning a 4-2 victory over Raleigh. He would go on to join the New York Giants as an outfielder in 1913.

BIRTHDAYS:

Wally Joyner, 1962; Chris Gomez, 1971; Kerry Wood, 1977; Dewon Brazelton, 1980

TRIVIA:

Thorpe won both the pentathlon and the decathlon at the 1912 Olympics. But when it was discovered he'd played ball in the minors for $60 a game, violating his amateur status, he was forced to return his Olympic medals. Thirty years after his death, however, his name was cleared and his medals were restored.

QUIZ:

This All-American basketball star at Duke played briefly for the NBA's Pistons and then moved on to baseball, where, as a member of the champion Pirates, he was named the 1960 NL MVP. Name him.

ANSWER: *Dick Groat*

TODAY'S THOUGHT:

"If there ever was a man to be born a hitter it was me."
—*Ted Williams*

HISTORY:

On this date in 1970 Willie Mays, with 615 homers, and Ernie Banks, with 504, both went deep in a Giants-Cubs matchup at Candlestick Park. It marked the first time two big leaguers with 500 home runs teed off in the same game.

BIRTHDAY:

Dave Concepcion, 1948

TRIVIA:

A couple of the guys with the "right stuff" participated together in U.S. bombing missions over Korea. Co-piloting with Hall of Famer Ted Williams was astronaut John Glenn.

EXTRA INNING:

"If the world were perfect, it wouldn't be." –*Yogi Berra*

QUIZ:

Who holds the record for most RBIs in a World Series?

ANSWER: *Bobby Richardson of the Yankees drove in twelve runs in the 1960 World Series.*

TODAY'S THOUGHT:

"I told you we'd improve our bench." —*Jack McKeon*, on renovation of the San Diego dugout

HISTORY:

On this date in 1960 Tom Sheehan became the oldest man to make his big league managerial debut- doing so with the San Francisco Giants following the firing of Bill Rigney. Sheehan, who was 66 years, 2 months, and 18 days old, would finish the season, leading the Giants to a 46-50 record.

BIRTHDAYS:

Lou Brock, 1939; Andres Galarraga, 1961; Sandy Alomar Jr., 1966; Felix Heredia, 1975

TRIVIA:

In 2003, 72 year-old Jack McKeon became the oldest manager to win a World Series when his Florida Marlins defeated the New York Yankees in six games.

QUIZ:

Who is the only manager to lead four different teams to division crowns?

ANSWER: *Billy Martin, who won division titles with the Yankees (1976, '77), Twins ('69), Tigers ('72) and A's ('81)*

TODAY'S THOUGHT:

"There are three things the average man thinks he can do better than anyone else: build a fire, run a hotel and manage a baseball team." —*Rocky Bridges*

HISTORY:

On this date in 1927 the Phillies' Jack Scott became the last of the "ironmen" when he pitched complete games of both ends of a doubleheader, winning the opener but losing the nightcap against the Reds.

BIRTHDAYS:

Lou Gehrig, 1903; Doug Mientkiewicz, 1974

TRIVIA:

The 1920 White Sox and the 1971 Orioles are the only teams in history to have four 20-game winners in the same season.

EXTRA INNING:

"Airplanes may kill you, but they ain't likely to hurt you." –*Satchel Paige*

QUIZ:

What former Boston player and Cy Young Award winner co-authored *The Bronx Zoo*?

ANSWER: *Sparky Lyle*

TODAY'S THOUGHT:

"All I'm asking for is what I want." —*Rickey Henderson*

HISTORY:

On this date in 1901 the Pirates' Honus Wagner became the first twentieth century player to steal home twice in a single game, as the Pittsburgh Pirates defeated the New York Giants, 7-0.

BIRTHDAYS:

Dickie Thon, 1958; Rob Mackowiak, 1976; Carlos Lee, 1976

TRIVIA:

Rickey Henderson was the first player to have two consecutive seasons (1982 and '83) with more than 100 stolen bases. Two years later, Vince Coleman became the first to do it in three straight seasons (1985, '86, and '87 - the first three years of his career).

QUIZ:

Five players in major league history have stolen over 800 bases. How many can you name?

ANSWER: *Rickey Henderson (1,406 steals), Lou Brock (938), Billy Hamilton (912), Ty Cobb (892) and Tim Raines (808)*

TODAY'S THOUGHT:

"On Father's Day, we again wish you all happy birthday."
—*Ralph Kiner*

HISTORY:

On this date in 1964 Jim Bunning, a father of ten, celebrated Father's Day by throwing a perfect game, 6-0, against the Mets.

BIRTHDAYS:

Ed Lopat, 1918; Rick Sutcliffe, 1956

TRIVIA:

Bunning and Nolan Ryan are the only pitchers to have thrown no-hitters in both the American and National Leagues.

EXTRA INNING:

"That's too bad; they're the only team I can beat." –*Dave Cole*, on being traded to the Phillies in the mid-1950's

QUIZ:

What pitcher appeared in the most games over any five-year span?

ANSWER: *Kent Tekulve appeared in 399 games from 1976-80 and finished his career with 1,050 games, all in relief.*

TODAY'S THOUGHT:

"Tonight, we're honoring one of the all-time greats in baseball, Stan Musial. He's immoral." —*Johnny Logan*, ex-major leaguer, introducing Musial at a banquet

HISTORY:

On this date in 1962 the Cardinals' Stan Musial, with two hits in one inning, passed Ty Cobb for the most career total bases. The 41-year-old Musial tied Cobb's record of 5,863 bases with a home run, and later in the inning, hit a two-run single for the record-breaker.

BIRTHDAYS:

Carl Hubbell, 1903; Willie Harris, 1978; Brad Hawpe, 1979

TRIVIA:

Hank Aaron now holds the total base record, with 6,858. He also holds the major league marks for most RBIs (2,297) and extra-base hits (1,477), and ranks second all-time in at-bats (12,364) and runs - tied with Babe Ruth (2,174).

QUIZ:

Who was the last National League player to bat .400 for a season?

ANSWER: *New York Giants first baseman Bill Terry hit .401 in 1930.*

TODAY'S THOUGHT:

"Baseball gives you every chance to be great. Then it puts every pressure on you to prove you haven't got what it takes."
—Joe Garagiola

HISTORY:

On this date in 1971 Philadelphia's Rick Wise became the answer to a trivia question, becoming the only pitcher to hit two home runs while recording a no-hitter.

BIRTHDAYS:

George Weiss, 1894; Tom Haller, 1937; Mark Hendrickson, 1974

TRIVIA:

Earl Wilson is the only other pitcher to hit a home run while pitching a no-hitter in the same game.

EXTRA INNING:

"Listen up, because I've got nothing to say and I'm only going to say it once." –*Yogi Berra*

QUIZ:

What team won 101 games in 1961 and still finished eight games back in the standings?

ANSWER: *The Detroit Tigers were 101-61, but the New York Yankees, led by Roger Maris and Mickey Mantle, went 109-53.*

TODAY'S THOUGHT:

"First snow this morning and now this. I feel cheated." — *Reds owner Marge Schott*, after umpire John McSherry's death on the field forced the postponement of the Reds' season opener in 1996

HISTORY:

On this date in 1882 Richard Higham became the first major league umpire banned from the game for cheating. Higham was accused of conspiring to help throw a Detroit Wolverines game and, ultimately, found guilty of collusion with gamblers.

BIRTHDAY:

George Harper, 1892

TRIVIA:

Before 1859, baseball umpires sat comfortably behind home plate in padded rocking chairs.

QUIZ:

In the 1985 World Series, what umpire appeared to blow a game six, ninth-inning call that may have cost the St. Louis Cardinals the championship?

ANSWER: *Don Denkinger - With the Cards up 1-0, the Royals' Jorge Orta hit a grounder towards first and seemed to be out by a step. Denkinger called him safe. Kansas City rallied to win the game, and, the next day the Series.*

TODAY'S THOUGHT:

"I think of myself as 'catching' the ball with my bat and letting the pitcher supply the power." —*Barry Bonds*

HISTORY:

On this date in 1968 Giants rookie Bobby Bonds, in his third major league at bat, hit a grand slam off Dodgers pitcher John Purdin. Bonds was the first and only twentieth century player to hit a bases-loaded home run in his big league debut.

BIRTHDAYS:

Mike Stanley, 1963; Aaron Sele, 1970; Michael Tucker, 1971; Carlos Delgado, 1972; Aramis Ramirez, 1978

TRIVIA:

Bobby and Barry Bonds are the only father-son tandem who are members of the 30/30 club (home runs/stolen bases in a single season).

QUIZ:

Were umpires once referred to as "Diamond Dicks" or "Blind Basemen"?

ANSWER: *Diamond Dicks*

TODAY'S THOUGHT:

"There's somebody warming up in the bullpen, but he's obscured by his number." —*Jerry Coleman*

HISTORY:

On this date in 1916 the Cleveland Indians became the first major league team to wear numbers on their uniforms. The Tribe wore the numerals on their left sleeves, but would abandon the idea the following year.

BIRTHDAYS:

Abner Doubleday, 1819; Babe Herman, 1903; Jeff Conine, 1966; Mike Myers, 1969; Jason Kendall, 1974; Derek Jeter, 1974; Chris Shelton, 1980

TRIVIA:

The concept of having numbers on uniforms took a long time to catch on. It would be thirteen years before any other team adopted the idea, when the Yankees joined the Indians in wearing numbers on the backs of their jerseys.

QUIZ:

The Cleveland Indians have retired the number 455. Why?

ANSWER: *The number is in honor of Cleveland's fans. From June of 1995 until April of 2001, the Indians sold out 455 consecutive games at Jacobs Field, a major league record.*

TODAY'S THOUGHT:

"Defense is baseball's visible poetry, and its invisible virtue."
—*Thomas Boswell*

HISTORY:

On this date in 2003 the Boston Red Sox set a major league record by scoring 10 runs before the first out. The 50-minute, 91-pitch first inning came during a 25–8 win over the Marlins. Two AL marks were tied when the Sox plated 14 runs in the inning, and Johnny Damon stroked three hits.

BIRTHDAYS:

Gus Zernial, 1923; Jim Edmonds, 1970; Daryl Ward, 1975; Johnny Estrada, 1976

TRIVIA:

Damon's single, double, and triple in the inning equaled the mark set in 1953 by Gene Stephens, then a Red Sox rookie. Stephens' Sox scored 17 runs in the seventh inning of a 23-3 win over the Tigers.

QUIZ:

Who is the only man in major league history to homer in his first and last plate appearances?

ANSWER: *John Miller, with the Yankees in 1966, and three years later with the Dodgers - The two home runs were also the only ones he hit in his career.*

TODAY'S THOUGHT:

"They shouldn't throw at me. I'm the father of five or six kids."
—*Tito Fuentes*, after getting hit by a pitch

HISTORY:

On this date in 1987 Don Baylor received a birthday gift he probably could have done without. Baylor was hit by a pitch for the 244th time, breaking the career record set by Ron Hunt. Baylor's record has since been broken by Craig Biggio.

BIRTHDAYS:

Ken Williams, 1890; Al Downing, 1941; Don Baylor, 1949; Mark Grace, 1964; Corey Koskie, 1973; Richard Hidalgo, 1975; Brandon Phillips, 1981

TRIVIA:

Baylor reached the World Series three times in his career as a player. Oddly enough, they came in consecutive years with three different teams—the Red Sox in 1986, the Twins in '87, and the A's in '88. He won his lone championship with Minnesota in 1987.

QUIZ:

Don Baylor was the first-ever manager for what major league franchise?

ANSWER: *Colorado Rockies, from 1993-98*

TODAY'S THOUGHT:

"Show me a good loser and I'll show you an idiot."
—*Leo Durocher*

HISTORY:

On this date in 1984 the Expos' Pete Rose, facing off against his former team, the Reds, became Major League Baseball's all-time leader in games played when he appeared in his 3,309th, surpassing Carl Yastrzemski.

BIRTHDAYS:

Harmon Killebrew, 1936; Pedro Guerrero, 1956

TRIVIA:

In 1998, while playing with the Triple A Indianapolis Indians, Pete Rose, Jr., had a part in a rare "home run cycle." In the same inning Rose opened with a solo shot, three teammates followed with a three-run homer, a grand slam, and a two-run dinger.

QUIZ:

The number 29 has been retired by two teams for what player?

ANSWER: *Rod Carew, by the Twins and Angels*

TODAY'S THOUGHT:

"The Mets have gotten their leadoff hitter on base only once this inning." —*Ralph Kiner*

HISTORY:

On this date in 1908 Cy Young pitched his third career no-hitter as the Red Sox defeated the New York Highlanders, 8-0. The 41-year-old Young not only drove in four runs for Boston, but barely missed out on his second perfect game, walking just one batter - leadoff hitter Harry Niles.

BIRTHDAYS:

Bud Black, 1957; Tony Fernandez, 1962; Mark Grudzielanek, 1970; Garrett Anderson, 1972; Chan Ho Park, 1973

TRIVIA:

Nolan Ryan topped Cy Young by throwing two no-hitters after the age of 40. At 43, he threw no-hitter number six against the A's. Less than a year later, he threw number seven against the Blue Jays, breaking his own record.

QUIZ:

Who was the first pitcher to win at least one game against every present-day team?

ANSWER: *Al Leiter*

TODAY'S THOUGHT:

"There is no more beautiful sight than a ballpark full of people."
—*White Sox owner Bill Veeck*

HISTORY:

On this date in 1910 Chicago's Comiskey Park opened its gates for the first time. It would be home to the White Sox until 1991, when the new Comiskey Park (later named US Cellular Field) became the friendly confines.

BIRTHDAYS:

Roger Connor, 1857; John Clarkson, 1861

TRIVIA:

Coincidentally, on Comiskey's 80th birthday, Yankees hurler Andy Hawkins threw a no-hitter, but lost to the White Sox, 4-0.

EXTRA INNING:

"The workout is optional. Whoever doesn't come gets optioned."
–*Bobby Valentine*

QUIZ:

Who had the only 40 homer/.400 batting average season in baseball history?

ANSWER: *Rogers Hornsby - Hornsby hit .401 with 42 homers in 1922.*

TODAY'S THOUGHT:

"The whole art of pitching is in the wrist." —*Carl Hubbell*

HISTORY:

On this date in 1933 Giants pitcher Carl Hubbell pitched an 18-inning shutout against the Cardinals. In the following game of the doubleheader, the Giants' Roy Parmelee struck out 13 and again held the Cards scoreless. St. Louis lost both games 1-0 and went an amazing 27 innings without touching home.

BIRTHDAYS:

Tony Armas, 1953; Jose Canseco, 1964; Steve Sparks, 1965; So Taguchi, 1969; Sean Casey, 1974

TRIVIA:

Carl Hubbell holds the record for the most consecutive pitching wins, with 24. The streak lasted over ten months from 1936 to '37. Because of his reliability on the mound, Hubbell earned the nickname, "Meal Ticket."

QUIZ:

Thinking big: Who were "The Big Six," "The Big Train" and "The Big Cat?"

ANSWER: *Christy Mathewson, Walter Johnson and Johnny Mize*

TODAY'S THOUGHT:

"I'm probably the only guy who worked for Stengel before and after he was a genius." —*Warren Spahn*, on having played for manager Casey Stengel with the losing Braves and Mets, but not for the Ol' Perfesser's championship years with the Yankees

HISTORY:

On this date in 1966 Tony Cloninger of the Atlanta Braves became the first National League player, let alone pitcher, ever to hit two grand slams in one game. His nine RBIs also set a major league mark for pitchers, as Atlanta routed the San Francisco Giants, 17-3.

BIRTHDAYS:

Frank Tanana, 1953; Greg Vaughn, 1965; Moises Alou, 1966

TRIVIA:

Charles Dillon Stengel got the nickname "Casey" from his birthplace, Kansas City ("KC"), Missouri.

QUIZ:

Who played in the most regular season baseball games without appearing in a postseason contest?

ANSWER: *Ernie Banks, 2,528 games*

TODAY'S THOUGHT:

"Whoever wants to know the heart and mind of America had better learn baseball."
—*Jacques Barzun*, philosophy professor

HISTORY:

On this date in 1939 Lou Gehrig bid farewell to his teammates and a crowd of over 61,000 at Yankee Stadium with an emotional speech in which he called himself "the luckiest man on the face of the earth."

BIRTHDAYS:

Mickey Welch, 1859; George Mullin, 1880; Chuck Tanner, 1929; George Steinbrenner, 1930; Vinny Castilla, 1967; Brendan Donnelly, 1971

TRIVIA:

Gehrig and Babe Ruth feuded for six years, not speaking to each other. The silence was broken when the two embraced and spoke at the Yankee Stadium ceremony.

QUIZ:

Fourteen players, including Lou Gehrig, have hit four homers in a single major league game. Two players did this in 2002. Who were they?

ANSWER: *The Mariners' Mike Cameron and the Dodgers' Shawn Green*

TODAY'S THOUGHT:

"He was a great American, he served the country in World War II, and was a great ball player. He was kind of like Buzz Aldrin, the second man to the moon, because he was the second African-American man in the majors." —*Bob Feller*, on Larry Doby

HISTORY:

On this date in 1947 twenty-two year-old Larry Doby became the first black American League player when he pinch-hit and struck out for the Cleveland Indians in a 6-5 loss against the Chicago White Sox.

BIRTHDAYS:

Tim Worrell, 1967; Goose Gossage, 1951; Jesse Crain, 1981

TRIVIA:

As a seventeen year-old, Doby joined the Newark Eagles of the Negro League, playing under the name Larry Walker. Like many college athletes, he used a pseudonym to protect his amateur status.

QUIZ:

What two players share the major league record for most pinch-hit home runs in a season?

ANSWER: *Dave Hansen (2000) and Craig Wilson (2001), with 7 each*

TODAY'S THOUGHT:

"The 1930s saw an effort to apply the principles of business to baseball, especially in the area of advertising and promotional techniques. The first major breakthrough came in 1933 with the institution of the All-Star Game." *—Richard Crepeau*

HISTORY:

On this date in 1933 players from the National League and the American League squared off at Comiskey Park for baseball's first All-Star Game. Babe Ruth's two-run home run led the AL to a 4-2 victory.

BIRTHDAYS:

Steve O'Neill, 1891; Willie Randolph, 1954; Lance Johnson, 1963

TRIVIA:

The first All-Star Game was planned as part of the festivities for the Chicago World's Fair. Proceeds from the game went to charity.

EXTRA INNING:

"I was due for a bad outing." –Bill Bonham, pitcher, after failing to retire any batters in his first major league game

QUIZ:

Who hit the first grand slam in All-Star Game history?

ANSWER: *Fred Lynn of the California Angels, who hit it exactly 50 years after the inaugural All-Star contest, on the same day and in the same park*

TODAY'S THOUGHT:

"He is not a dog; a dog is loyal and runs after the ball."
—*Tommy Lasorda*, on Daryl Strawberry

HISTORY:

On this date in 1936 the National League All-Stars, thanks to six shutout innings by the combo of Dizzy Dean and Carl Hubbell, won their first midsummer classic. The Nationals edged the Americans, 4-3, at Braves Field in Boston.

BIRTHDAYS:

Satchel Paige, 1907; Billy Herman, 1909; Dan Gladden, 1957; Dave Burba, 1966; Chuck Knoblauch, 1968; Matt Mantei, 1973

TRIVIA:

The All-Star Game was dreamed up by *Chicago Tribune* sports editor Arch Ward.

QUIZ:

Who was the first major leaguer to make the All-Star team as a catcher and then a second baseman?

ANSWER: *Craig Biggio of the Houston Astros made the squad as a catcher in 1991 and then as a second baseman a year later.*

TODAY'S THOUGHT:

"The only bad thing about winning the pennant is that you have to manage the All-Star Game the next year. I'd rather go fishing for three days." —*Whitey Herzog*

HISTORY:

On this date in 1941 Ted Williams' three-run home run with two outs in the ninth inning off Claude Passeau gave the American League a thrilling 7-5 All-Star Game victory in Detroit.

BIRTHDAYS:

Ken Sanders, 1941; Terry Puhl, 1956

TRIVIA:

The 1941 All-Star Game also featured Joe and Dom DiMaggio, both playing for the American League. The brothers were the first ever to appear in the same All-Star contest.

EXTRA INNING:

"We'll do all right if we capitalize on our mistakes." –Yankee outfielder *Mickey Rivers*

QUIZ:

Who was the first player to win the All-Star and regular season MVP Awards in the same year?

ANSWER: *Maury Wills, in 1962*

TODAY'S THOUGHT:

"I'm in the twilight of a mediocre career." —*Frank Sullivan*, former Phillies pitcher

HISTORY:

On this date in 2002 despite chants of "Let them play!" from the sellout crowd in Milwaukee, Commissioner Bud Selig called the All-Star Game a 7-7 tie after 11 innings because of a lack of bench players.

BIRTHDAY:

Willie Wilson, 1955

TRIVIA:

The 2002 game was to have featured the first annual Ted Williams Most Valuable Player Award. Because of the circumstances, no one received it.

EXTRA INNING:

""Don't fail to miss tomorrow's game." –*Dizzy Dean*, on the air

QUIZ:

Between 1959 and 1962 the major leagues played two All-Star Games a year. In '59, what National League hurler started both games?

ANSWER: *The Dodgers' Don Drysdale*

TODAY'S THOUGHT:

"I don't really go to compete. I go to be seen."
—*Reggie Jackson*, on his All-Star Game appearances

HISTORY:

On this date in 1934 the National League's Carl Hubbell fanned Babe Ruth, Lou Gehrig, Jimmie Foxx, Al Simmons, and Joe Cronin consecutively in the second All-Star Game. The AL, however, rallied from a 4-0 deficit to win, 9-7.

BIRTHDAYS:

Hal McRae, 1945; Andre Dawson, 1954; Marty Cordova, 1969

TRIVIA:

In the 1934 All-Star Game, 17 of the 18 players who started the game were eventually inducted into the Hall of Fame. The lone non-Hall of Famer was National League centerfielder Wally Berger.

QUIZ:

Besides Carl Hubbell, what other pitcher has fanned five consecutive batters in an All-Star Game?

ANSWER: *Fernando Valenzuela of the National League fanned Don Mattingly, Cal Ripken, Jr., Jesse Barfield, Lou Whitaker and Ted Higuera in 1986.*

TODAY'S THOUGHT:

"Ryan is the only guy who puts fear in me. Not because he can get you out, but because he can kill you." —*Reggie Jackson*

HISTORY:

On this date in 1985 Nolan Ryan fanned the Mets' Danny Heep to become the first pitcher to reach 4,000 strikeouts. Ryan finished with 11 Ks in seven innings of work as his Astros won, 4-3, in 12 innings.

BIRTHDAY:

Andy Ashby, 1967

TRIVIA:

Cesar Geronimo was the 3,000th strikeout victim of both Nolan Ryan and Bob Gibson.

EXTRA INNING:

"One of my goals in life was to be surrounded by unpretentious, rich young men. Then I bought the Braves and I was surrounded by 25 of them." –*Ted Turner*

QUIZ:

Name the three Giants players who were Rookies of the Year in the 1950's.

ANSWER: *Willie Mays, Orlando Cepeda and Willie McCovey*

TODAY'S THOUGHT:

"He enjoyed people enjoying themselves. He was color-blind and race-blind and religious-blind."
—*Hank Greenberg*, on Bill Veeck

HISTORY:

On this date in 1979 the Chicago White Sox held a Disco Demolition Night, promoted by owner Bill Veeck, where people brought unwanted disco records to Comiskey Park in exchange for a small admission fee. Between games of the doubleheader, fans raced onto the field and rioted for over an hour, causing the Sox to forfeit the nightcap to the Tigers.

BIRTHDAYS:

Lee Meadows, 1894; Ron Fairly, 1938; Kelly Wunsch, 1972

TRIVIA:

In 1995, the Class A Durham Bulls sponsored a Strike Out Domestic Violence Night. The event, however, became a disaster when Earl Nelson of the Bulls kicked a member of the opposing team in the groin and head to begin a half-hour brawl between the two teams.

QUIZ:

What catcher reversed his jersey number when he went from the Red Sox to the White Sox?

ANSWER: *Carlton Fisk, who wore "27" on his uniform in Boston, switched to "72" in Chicago.*

TODAY'S THOUGHT:

"I have the right to knock down anybody holding a bat."
—*Early Wynn*

HISTORY:

On this date in 1963 Cleveland pitcher Early Wynn joined the 300 victory club when he pitched the Indians to a 7-4 victory over the Kansas City A's.

BIRTHDAYS:

Stan Coveleski, 1889; Yadier Molina, 1982

TRIVIA:

New York Yankees outfielder Gene Woodling homered off Early Wynn of the Cleveland Indians on June 24, July 24, and August 24, 1951.

EXTRA INNING:

"All I said was that the trades were stupid and dumb, and they took that and blew it all out of proportion." –*Ron Davis*, Twins pitcher, objecting to a newspaper story in which he criticized Minnesota's front office for trading away some of their better talent

QUIZ:

Can you name the Cleveland skipper who led the Indians to 111 wins in 1954?

ANSWER: *Al Lopez*

TODAY'S THOUGHT:

"If Pete Rose's streak was still intact, with that single to left, the fans would be throwing babies out of the upper deck."
—*Jerry Coleman*

HISTORY:

On this date in 1970 before a hometown Cincinnati crowd, Pete Rose crashed into Cleveland catcher Ray Fosse in the 12th inning of the 41st All-Star Game, breaking a 4-4 tie as well as Fosse's shoulder.

BIRTHDAYS:

Robin Ventura, 1967; Jose Hernandez, 1969; Tim Hudson, 1975

TRIVIA:

Ray Fosse's career was never the same after suffering the shoulder injury in the collision. The following season his batting average fell by 31 points to .276 and, by 1973, Fosse was hitting in the .100s. He was out of the league by age 32.

QUIZ:

On July 14, 1967, Eddie Mathews joined the 500 home run club. A year later, Hank Aaron did the same thing. What clubs were they playing for?

ANSWER: *Mathews was playing for the Houston Astros, while Aaron was still with the Atlanta Braves.*

TODAY'S THOUGHT:

"I've been asked this question a lot, 'How do you want to be remembered?' and my response to that question has been, 'To be remembered at all is pretty special.'" —*Cal Ripken, Jr.*

HISTORY:

On this date in 1980 and 1993 two home run records for position players were broken. In 1980, the Reds' Johnny Bench hit his 315th homer as a catcher, surpassing Yogi Berra. Thirteen years later, the Orioles' Cal Ripken, Jr., hit his 278th homer as a shortstop, moving past the Cubs' Ernie Banks.

BIRTHDAY:

Donn Clendenon, 1935

TRIVIA:

Mike Piazza, who has passed Bench on the all-time home run list, became the first catcher with 30 or more homers in his rookie season. Piazza hit 35 round-trippers in 1993 with the Dodgers.

QUIZ:

Only three shortstops in major league history have won six or more consecutive Gold Glove Awards. Name them.

ANSWER: *Mark Belanger, Ozzie Smith and Omar Vizquel*

TODAY'S THOUGHT:

"We've got a guy on our team who has such bad hands his glove is embarrassed." —*Frank Sullivan*

HISTORY:

On this date in 1897 Chicago's Cap Anson, at the age of 45, became the first major leaguer to reach 3,000 hits when he singled off Baltimore's George Blackburn.

BIRTHDAYS:

Shoeless Joe Jackson, 1887; Terry Pendleton, 1960

TRIVIA:

In 1885, Art Irwin became the first infielder to wear a glove. Irwin developed the first known fielder's mitt after padding a buckskin glove to protect his two broken fingers. Irwin patented the idea once it caught on.

QUIZ:

Identify these Hall of Famers by their nicknames: " The Commerce Comet," "The Flying Dutchman" and "The Rajah."

ANSWER: *Mickey Mantle, Honus Wagner and Rogers Hornsby*

TODAY'S THOUGHT:

"Always try for perfection. There's never been a perfect ballplayer. Willie Mays came closest, but always try." —*Joe DiMaggio*

HISTORY:

On this date in 1941 Cleveland held Joe DiMaggio hitless in three at bats ending his consecutive games hit streak at 56, the longest in Major League Baseball history. After the streak was halted, DiMaggio went on to hit in 16 more games in a row.

BIRTHDAY:

Jason Jennings, 1978

TRIVIA:

Joe's brother Dom hit in 34 straight games as a member of the Boston Red Sox in 1949. The team who stopped his streak - the New York Yankees.

QUIZ:

Phillies great Mike Schmidt was voted starting NL third baseman for the 1989 All-Star Game but didn't play. Why?

ANSWER: *He retired before the game.*

TODAY'S THOUGHT:

"It's deja vu all over again." —*Yogi Berra*

HISTORY:

On this date in 1999 David Cone threw the sixteenth perfect game in major league history, a 6-0 New York win over the Montreal Expos at Yankee Stadium.

BIRTHDAYS:

Johnny Hopp, 1916; Joe Torre, 1940; Donald Fehr, 1948; Mike Greenwell, 1963; Torii Hunter, 1975; Ben Sheets, 1978

TRIVIA:

Cone's perfect game couldn't have come on a more perfect day. Before the game, the Yankees honored Yogi Berra, who caught the first pitch from Don Larsen. Forty-three years earlier, with Berra behind the plate, Larsen pitched the only perfect game in World Series history against the Brooklyn Dodgers.

QUIZ:

Don Larsen and David Wells are tied together in Yankee history for their perfect games. But what other connection do they share?

ANSWER: *Both attended Point Loma High School in San Diego.*

TODAY'S THOUGHT:

"He can throw all day within a two-inch space, in, out, up or down. I've never seen anyone as good as that."
—*Hank Aaron*, on Juan Marichal

HISTORY:

On this date in 1960 Hall of Famer Juan Marichal made his debut for the San Francisco Giants shutting out the Philadelphia Phillies, 2-0. Marichal allowed only one single while throwing twelve strikeouts.

BIRTHDAYS:

Bob Meusel, 1896; Preston Wilson, 1974; Rick Ankiel, 1979

TRIVIA:

Marichal's son-in-law is former World Series MVP Jose Rijo.

EXTRA INNING:

"I've been a DH all my life. A designated Hebrew." –Baseball's first designated hitter, *Ron Blomberg*

QUIZ:

Who is the only major league pitcher with more than 100 career shutouts?

ANSWER: *Walter Johnson of the Washington Senators, with 110*

TODAY'S THOUGHT:

"Say this much for big league baseball- it is beyond question the greatest conversation piece ever invented in America."
—*Bruce Catton*, historian

HISTORY:

On this date in 1973 the Chicago White Sox' Wilbur Wood became the last hurler to start both halves of a doubleheader, losing both games to the Yankees, 12-2 and 7-0.

BIRTHDAYS:

Heinie Manush, 1901; Tony Oliva, 1940; Mike Witt, 1960; Charles Johnson, 1971; Bengie Molina, 1974

TRIVIA:

In 1973, Wilbur Wood was not only a 20 game winner - he was a 20 game loser. His rare pitching record for the season was 24-20.

QUIZ:

In 2001, what pitcher became the oldest first-time 20-game winner in major league history?

ANSWER: *Jamie Moyer, who at age 38 went 20-6 with the Mariners*

TODAY'S THOUGHT:

"Guys who can field you can shake out of any old tree. Find me guys who can hit." —*Rogers Hornsby*

HISTORY:

On this date in 1975 Mets infielder Joe Torre became the first player in National League history to hit into four straight double plays in a game. Felix Millan made it all possible, with four consecutive singles batting in front of Torre against the Astros.

BIRTHDAYS:

Dave Henderson, 1958; Mike Bordick, 1965; C.C. Sabathia, 1980

TRIVIA:

In 1965, Joe Torre, Eddie Mathews, Hank Aaron, and Gene Oliver each hit 10th-inning home runs, setting a record for the most homers in an extra inning, as the Braves won, 8–2, at Chicago.

QUIZ:

Who hit into the most double plays in major league history?

ANSWER: *Brooks Robinson, 618*

TODAY'S THOUGHT:

"The Senators were never very good, but not much has changed in Washington. The senators they have there still aren't very good." —*Richard Nixon*

HISTORY:

On this date in 1923 the Washington Senators' Walter Johnson became the first pitcher to strike out 3,000 batters when he fanned five in a 3-1 victory over the Cleveland Indians. He would finish his career with 3,508.

BIRTHDAYS:

Jack Glasscock, 1857; Doc Cramer, 1905; Sparky Lyle, 1944; Dave Stieb, 1957; Mike Sweeney, 1973; Scot Shields, 1975; Juan Uribe, 1979

TRIVIA:

Walter Johnson's final major league appearance came as a pinch hitter in the same game that Babe Ruth hit his then-record 60th home run of the season in 1927. Johnson, by the way, flew out to Ruth in his final at bat.

QUIZ:

What baseball Hall of Famer was the last manager of the Washington Senators?

ANSWER: *Ted Williams managed the Senators from 1969 to 1971. He then moved with the club to Texas, piloting the Rangers in 1972.*

TODAY'S THOUGHT:

"Just give me twenty five guys in the last year of their contract: I'll win a pennant every year." —*Sparky Anderson*

HISTORY:

On this date in 2000 first baseman Tony Perez and manager Sparky Anderson of the Big Red Machine were inducted into the Baseball Hall of Fame, along with 1975 World Series rival, Carlton Fisk.

BIRTHDAYS:

Pee Wee Reese, 1918, Don Drysdale, 1936; Nomar Garciaparra, 1973

TRIVIA:

Sparky Anderson is the only manager in All-Star Game history to suffer losses with both the American and National Leagues.

EXTRA INNING:

"Somebody else put their foot in my mouth for a change." –Seattle Mariners outfielder *Jay Buhner*, after taking a shot to the jaw while breaking up a double play

QUIZ:

Name the infielder who played in all 44 Yankees-Brooklyn Dodgers World Series games.

ANSWER: *Shortstop Pee Wee Reese of the Dodgers*

TODAY'S THOUGHT:

"If I stay healthy, I have a chance to collect 3,000 hits and 1,000 errors." —*George Brett*, near the end of his career

HISTORY:

On this date in 1983 George Brett's two-run, two out ninth-inning home run against the Yankees was disallowed when the umpires ruled that the pine tar on his bat went too far up the handle. The Yankees were granted a 4-3 victory before the decision was overturned by the league.

BIRTHDAYS:

Tommy McCarthy, 1863; Jack Clements, 1964; Barry Bonds, 1964

TRIVIA:

Because the Royals protest was upheld, the game was picked up on August 18, from the point of Brett's two-run home run. With only about 1,000 fans on hand, Kansas City reliever Dan Quisenberry closed out the 5-4 Royals win in twelve minutes.

QUIZ:

What pitcher yielded Brett's home run in the infamous "pine tar incident"?

ANSWER: *Yankee reliever Rich "Goose" Gossage*

TODAY'S THOUGHT:

"His fastball was so fast that by the time you'd made up your mind whether it would be a strike or not, it just wasn't there anymore." —*Charlie Gehringer*, on Lefty Grove

HISTORY:

On this date in 1941 forty-one year-old Boston Red Sox pitcher Lefty Grove recorded his 300th, and final, career victory when he defeated the Cleveland Indians, 10-6, at Fenway Park.

BIRTHDAYS:

Doug Drabek, 1962; Billy Wagner, 1971; Javier Vazquez, 1976

TRIVIA:

Lefty Grove is one of only two pitchers who gave up both a home run to Babe Ruth during the Babe's 60- home run season in 1927 and a hit to Joe DiMaggio during his 56-game hit streak in 1941. Ted Lyons of the White Sox is the other.

QUIZ:

What was the last team lefty Warren Spahn played for in his Hall of Fame career?

ANSWER: *The San Francisco Giants in 1965*

TODAY'S THOUGHT:

"The coldest winter I ever spent was a summer in San Francisco." —*Charlie Dressen*

HISTORY:

On this date in 1933 Joe DiMaggio, an 18-year-old playing in his first semi-pro season with the San Francisco Seals, saw his minor league record 61-game hitting streak come to an end during a Pacific Coast League game against Oakland.

BIRTHDAYS:

Sam Jones, 1892; Hoyt Wilhelm, 1923; Joaquin Benoit, 1977; Jason Botts, 1980

TRIVIA:

Ty Cobb holds the major league record for the most batting titles, with 12. Cobb hit .420 in 1911, and led the AL in hitting every year from 1907 to 1919, except 1916, when Tris Speaker took the crown by batting .386.

QUIZ:

In 1955 I became the youngest player to win a batting title. Who am I?

ANSWER: *Al Kaline, at age 20, batted .340 for the Detroit Tigers. He also contributed 27 home runs and 102 RBIs.*

TODAY'S THOUGHT:

"   " —*Steve Carlton*, who refused to talk to the media

HISTORY:

On this date in 1983 Gaylord Perry earned his first win with the Kansas City Royals, and became the fourth pitcher to reach 3,500 career strikeouts. Nolan Ryan and Steve Carlton had reached the milestone earlier in the season.

BIRTHDAYS:

Joe Tinker, 1880; Leo Durocher, 1905; Tom Goodwin, 1968; Alex Rodriguez, 1975; Shea Hillenbrand, 1975

TRIVIA:

Gaylord Perry's uniform number 36 was retired by the San Francisco Giants in 2005. The only other number 36 to have been retired was worn by Robin Roberts of the Philadelphia Phillies.

QUIZ:

Gaylord Perry won two Cy Young Awards in the '70s - one in each league. Can you name the teams he played for?

ANSWER: *Indians (1972) and Padres (1978)*

TODAY'S THOUGHT:

"We've got a little problem here. Luis Tiant wants to use the bathroom, and it says no foreign objects on the toilet."
—*Graig Nettles*, on an airplane with his Cuban teammate

HISTORY:

On this date in 1991 Dennis Martinez, a 36-year-old Nicaraguan, became the first Latin American pitcher to hurl a perfect game in the majors as the Expos beat the Dodgers, 2-0.

BIRTHDAYS:

Freddie Fitzsimmons, 1901; Vida Blue, 1949

TRIVIA:

Ron Hassey was the catcher for Montreal that day. He was also behind the plate for Cleveland when the Indians' Len Barker threw a perfect game against Toronto in 1981.

QUIZ:

In 1995, Dennis Martinez became the last pitcher to face what Hall of Famer after breaking his jaw with a wild pitch?

ANSWER: *Kirby Puckett - He would develop glaucoma in his right eye and retire the next year.*

TODAY'S THOUGHT:

"I'm glad I don't play anymore. I couldn't learn all those handshakes." —*Phil Rizzuto*

HISTORY:

On this date in 1983 Steve Garvey's bid to top Lou Gehrig's consecutive-game streak ended at 1,207 games when he dislocated his thumb in a collision at home plate. Garvey's streak was a National League record.

BIRTHDAY:

Dan Driessen, 1951

TRIVIA:

The 1965 Dodgers featured the big league's first all-switch hitting infield: Wes Parker played first base, Jim Lefebvre was at second, Maury Wills at short, and Jim Gilliam at third.

QUIZ:

What team had the same nine batters go to the plate in an entire World Series?

ANSWER: *The 1976 Cincinnati Reds, the first year the DH rule was in effect, used Dan Driessen as their designated hitter.*

TODAY'S THOUGHT:

"A lot of good ballgames on tomorrow, but we're going to be right here with the Cubs and the Mets." —*Thom Brennaman*, Chicago Cubs broadcaster

HISTORY:

On this date in 1968 Washington Senators shortstop Ron Hansen turned in the first unassisted triple play in the major leagues in more than 41 years. Hansen didn't fare well at the plate, however, fanning four times against the Indians in a 10-1 Senators' loss.

BIRTHDAYS:

Casey Stengel, 1890; Bud Selig, 1934

TRIVIA:

In 1962, Mets catcher Joe Pignatano hit into a triple play in the eighth inning of a 5-1 loss to the Cubs. Not only was it Pignatano's final career at-bat, but his rally-killing play contributed to the historic 120th loss of New York's season.

QUIZ:

What Hall of Famer hit into four triple plays during his career?

ANSWER: *Brooks Robinson*

TODAY'S THOUGHT:

"I have discovered, in twenty years of moving around a ballpark, that the knowledge of the game is usually in inverse proportion to the price of the seats." —*Bill Veeck*

HISTORY:

On this date in 1954 the Braves' Joe Adcock, using a borrowed bat, hit four home runs in a single game. He added a double to set a then- major league mark with 18 total bases in a 15-7 win over the Dodgers at Ebbets Field.

BIRTHDAYS:

Curt Gowdy, 1919; Scott Bankhead, 1963

TRIVIA:

Joe Adcock was the first of three men to reach the distant bleachers in center field at New York's Polo Grounds. He hit a home run in 1953 that went an estimated 475 feet. Lou Brock and Hank Aaron are the only others to do it.

QUIZ:

Who is the only person to hit a major league home run and score an NFL touchdown in the same week?

ANSWER: *Deion Sanders, in 1989 with the Yankees and the Falcons*

TODAY'S THOUGHT:

"If you slid into bases head first for twenty years, you'd be ugly, too." —*Pete Rose*

HISTORY:

On this date in 1978 the Reds' Pete Rose had his 44-game hitting streak snapped in a 16-4 loss to the Braves. Rose went 0-for-4, striking out to end the game. His streak remains the second longest in major league history.

BIRTHDAYS:

Greg Jefferies, 1967; Shigetosi Hasegawa, 1968

TRIVIA:

Pete Rose was a seventeen-time all-star at five different positions: second base, left field, right field, third base, and first base.

EXTRA INNING:

"Maybe you can talk the other team into throwing to you underhanded." –*A.J. Van Slyke*, seven-year-old son of Andy Van Slyke, during Dad's batting slump

QUIZ:

With the exception of Yogi Berra, this player caught more World Series games than anyone else. Name him.

ANSWER: *Elston Howard, who was the catcher in 33 games in ten World Series. Berra caught 63 games.*

TODAY'S THOUGHT:

"Munson's not moody, he's just mean. When you're moody, you're nice sometimes." *—Sparky Lyle*

HISTORY:

On this date in 1979 Yankees catcher and team captain Thurman Munson died tragically at age 32 when the private plane he was piloting crashed at the Akron-Canton Airport in Ohio.

BIRTHDAYS:

Red Ames, 1882; Tim Wakefield, 1966; Grady Sizemore, 1982; Huston Street, 1983

TRIVIA:

In the 1976 World Series, Munson batted .529 and recorded six consecutive hits to tie a record set by Goose Goslin of the Washington Senators in 1925. Both teams lost the Series in those years.

EXTRA INNING:

"It's a beautiful day for a night game." *–Frankie Frisch*

QUIZ:

What number was the only one retired twice by the New York Yankees?

ANSWER: *Eight, in honor of catchers Yogi Berra and Bill Dickey*

TODAY'S THOUGHT:

"Don't look back. Something might be gaining on you."
—*Satchel Paige*

HISTORY:

On this date in 1948 ageless Negro League legend Satchel Paige made his major league debut, pitching seven innings and leading the Indians over the Senators, 5-3.

BIRTHDAYS:

Harry Heilmann, 1894; Troy Glaus, 1976

TRIVIA:

Harry "Slug" Heilman was an odd hitter. The Detroit Tigers slugger won the American League batting title every other year from 1921 to '27.

EXTRA INNING:

"It's like watching Mario Andretti park a car." –*Ralph Kiner*, on Phil Niekro's knuckleball

QUIZ:

Two center fielders have won back-to-back MVP Awards, one in the AL and one in the NL. Can you name them?

ANSWER: *Mickey Mantle of the Yankees (1956 & '57) and Dale Murphy of the Atlanta Braves (1982 & '83)*

TODAY'S THOUGHT:

"If you don't know where you're going, you could wind up someplace else." —*Yogi Berra*

HISTORY:

On this date in 1982 Joel Youngblood, traded from the Mets to the Expos, became the first major leaguer to get a hit for two different teams in two different cities (Chicago and Philadelphia) on the same day.

BIRTHDAYS:

Jake Beckley, 1867; Dallas Green, 1934; Cleon Jones, 1942; Roger Clemens, 1962; B.J. Surhoff, 1964; Troy O'Leary, 1969; Eric Milton, 1975

TRIVIA:

Eddie Mathews is the only man to play with the same team (Braves) in three different cities. He began his career in 1952, the Braves final year in Boston. He then played the club's entire 1953 to '65 stay in Milwaukee before playing one year, 1966, in Atlanta.

QUIZ:

With what team did Hall of Fame pitcher Steve Carlton finish his career?

ANSWER: *Carlton ended his career in 1988 with the Minnesota Twins.*

TODAY'S THOUGHT:

"The average attendance at Cubs games is 48 degrees."

—Harry Caray

HISTORY:

On this date in 2005 the Cardinals' Albert Pujols became the first player to hit 30 or more home runs in each of his first five major league seasons. For those five years, Pujols' total of 201 homers placed him second behind only Ralph Kiner's 215.

BIRTHDAYS:

John Olerud, 1968; Bobby Kielty, 1976; Mark Mulder, 1977; Eric Hinske, 1977; Carl Crawford, 1981

TRIVIA:

Frank Zupo and George Zuverink formed the only "Z" battery in major league history. The Z-boys twice formed a one-inning battery for the Baltimore Orioles in 1957.

QUIZ:

Who holds the record for most stolen bases in a season without being caught?

ANSWER: *Kevin McReynolds stole 21 bases without being thrown out while playing for the New York Mets in 1988.*

TODAY'S THOUGHT:

"Some people have a chip on their shoulder. Billy has a whole lumberyard." —*Jim Murray*, sportswriter, on Billy Martin

HISTORY:

On this day in 1988 Goose Gossage picked up his 300th career save in a 7-4 Cubs' win over Philadelphia, while Jose Canseco became the eleventh player to hit 30 home runs and steal 30 bases in a season as the A's beat Seattle, 5-4.

BIRTHDAYS:

Sherry Magee, 1884; Andy Messersmith, 1945; Ken Phelps, 1954; Victor Zambrano, 1975

TRIVIA:

Nine years earlier, as a player for the Reds, Billy Martin charged the mound after receiving a brushback pitch from Cubs pitcher Jim Brewer. Martin threw his bat at Brewer and punched him in the face. Brewer was hospitalized for two months with a broken jaw.

QUIZ:

Who has managed the Minnesota Twins for more seasons than anyone else?

ANSWER: *Tom Kelly, from 1986 to 2001*

TODAY'S THOUGHT:

"I've found that you don't need to wear a necktie if you can hit."
—*Ted Williams*

HISTORY:

On this date in 1956 Ted Williams was fined $5,000 by the Red Sox for spitting at the Fenway crowd. The incident came after fans booed him for dropping a fly ball in the eleventh inning against the Yankees. The Sox won when The Splendid Splinter walked with the bases loaded in the bottom of the inning.

BIRTHDAYS:

Bill McKechnie, 1886; Don Larsen, 1929; Danny Graves, 1973; Edgar Renteria, 1975

TRIVIA:

Willams gave his 1946 World Series check to the Red Sox clubhouse boy as a tip.

QUIZ:

Who was selected the 2004 Sportsman of the Year by *Sports Illustrated*?

ANSWER: *The Boston Red Sox team*

TODAY'S THOUGHT:

"Putting the lights on Wrigley Field is like putting aluminum siding on the Sistine Chapel." —*Roger Simon*, columnist

HISTORY:

On this date in 1988 the lights came on in Chicago when a 91-year-old fan flipped a switch turning on 540 stadium roof lights, as the Phillies and Cubs met in the first-ever night game at Wrigley Field.

BIRTHDAYS:

Cecil Travis, 1913; Frank Howard, 1936; Jose Cruz, 1947

TRIVIA:

The game was actually postponed after four innings due to rain, so the first "official" game in which lights were used at Wrigley came the following night when the Cubs beat the Mets, 6-4.

EXTRA INNING:

"My wife, so I can see how wonderful it is to live with myself." –*Andy Van Slyke*, when asked if there was anyone else in the world he would change places with for a day

QUIZ:

What two names was Wrigley Field formerly known as before 1926?

ANSWER: *Weeghman Park (1914-20) and Cubs Park (1920-25)*

TODAY'S THOUGHT:

"I've never questioned the integrity of an umpire. Their eyesight, yes." —*Leo Durocher*

HISTORY:

On this date in 1976 Cal Hubbard became a three-time Hall of Famer, after his enshrinement in Cooperstown as an umpire. He had previously been inducted into the College and Professional Halls of Fame in the early 1960's as a player.

BIRTHDAYS:

Bill Campbell, 1948; Ted Simmons, 1949; Deion Sanders, 1967; Troy Percival, 1969; Matt Morris, 1974; Brian Fuentes, 1975

TRIVIA:

A standout lineman in the National Football League for nine seasons, Hubbard was once the captain of the Green Bay Packers.

QUIZ:

Who hit more home runs as a third baseman than anyone in American League history?

ANSWER: *Craig Nettles, with 319*

TODAY'S THOUGHT:

"When I first fly, I wear blue suit and we no crash."
—*Mike Cuellar,* on why he always wore a blue suit while flying

HISTORY:

On this date in 1971 Minnesota Twin Harmon Killebrew became the tenth player in major league history to hit 500 home runs when he teed off against Orioles pitcher Mike Cuellar. Killebrew also hit number 501 in the Twins 4-3, ten-inning loss.

BIRTHDAYS:

Buddy Lewis, 1916; Rocky Colavito, 1933; Gerald Williams, 1966; Brandon Lyon, 1979; Dan Johnson, 1979

TRIVIA:

Mike "Crazy Legs" Cuellar was known for his many superstitions, like insisting that the baseball be sitting on the mound when he went out to pitch, and smoking a cigarette in the locker room hallway while the first hitter of every Baltimore inning batted.

QUIZ:

Aside from the number 42 that every team retired in honor of Jackie Robinson, the Twins have retired five numbers. Which ones?

ANSWER: 3 (*Harmon Killebrew*), 6 (*Tony Oliva*), 14 (*Kent Hrbek*), 29 (*Rod Carew*), and 34 (*Kirby Puckett*)

TODAY'S THOUGHT:

"My arm has felt so bad since I retired that I can't even throw a tantrum." —*Chicago Cubs broadcaster Steve Stone,* when asked if he would attempt a comeback

HISTORY:

On this date in 2003 the Cubs' Kerry Wood became the fastest major leaguer to reach the 1,000-strikeout mark after fanning the Astros' Jeff Kent. It took Wood just 134 games and 853 innings to reach the milestone, both records.

BIRTHDAYS:

Bill Monbouquette, 1936; Bryn Smith, 1955

TRIVIA:

There are eight holes on a standard wiffle ball.

EXTRA INNING:

"I always said I wanted to lead by example, but this is ridiculous."
–*Ken Howell,* the first of nine Phillies to go on the disabled list in one season

QUIZ:

Second-guessing: Pete Rose has played in the most games, 3,562. Who's second?

ANSWER: *Carl Yastrzemski,* 3,308

TODAY'S THOUGHT:

"Ballplayers and deerhunters are alike. They both want the big bucks." —*Larry Doughty*, former Pirates GM

HISTORY:

On this date in 1994 Major League Baseball players went on strike. The result was cancellation of the World Series for the first time in 90 years, as baseball became the first sport in history to lose its postseason to a labor dispute. The work stoppage was the eighth in baseball history and the third in 23 years.

BIRTHDAYS:

Christy Mathewson, 1880; Ray Schalk, 1892; Matt Clement, 1974; Lew Ford, 1976

TRIVIA:

When the 1994 season was cut short, the Montreal Expos held baseball's best record at 74-40, the best winning percentage in franchise history. However, it was decided that every team in '94 finished tied for last place, as the season was unofficial.

QUIZ:

What was the only team to finish with 70 losses in the strike-shortened season?

ANSWER: *The San Diego Padres, who went 47-70*

TODAY'S THOUGHT:

"Baseball is like church. Many attend, but few understand."
—*Wes Westrum*, San Francisco Giants coach

HISTORY:

On this date in 1969 acting commissioner of Major League Baseball Bowie Kuhn was formally appointed to the position. Kuhn's "temporary" assignment lasted until 1984.

BIRTHDAYS:

Sid Gordon, 1917; Mudcat Grant, 1935; Andre Thornton, 1949; Jay Buhner, 1964; Mark Lemke, 1965; Jarrod Washburn, 1974; Corey Patterson, 1979

TRIVIA:

Kuhn to this day is the youngest (42 years), tallest (6-foot-5) and heaviest (240 pounds) commissioner in baseball history.

EXTRA INNING:

"I'm not sure what it means, but when the ball is not in play, somebody grabs his crotch." –*Paula Bouton*

QUIZ:

What was Atlanta's Turner Field originally called?

ANSWER: *Centennial Olympic Stadium*

TODAY'S THOUGHT:

"It's more relaxed here. It's an atmosphere I can relate to. In Oakland it was always win, win, win and you get fed up with it."
—*Jose Canseco*, after his move to Texas

HISTORY:

On this date in 1987 Oakland A's rookie outfielder Mark McGwire hit his 39th homer of the year, off Don Sutton. That set a new record for home runs in a season by a rookie, a mark that McGwire would extend to 49.

BIRTHDAYS:

Cupid Childs, 1867; Earl Weaver, 1930; Mark Fidrych, 1954; Mark Loretta, 1971; Juan Pierre, 1977

TRIVIA:

One of the worst home-run hitters of all-time was Tommy Thevenow, who in 4,164 career at-bats, hit two homers. Both of Thevenow's home runs came in 1926 with the Cardinals, and both were inside-the-park.

QUIZ:

In 2006, who became the oldest player in major league history to hit a home run?

ANSWER: *Julio Franco, at 47 years and 240 days old, connected for a two-run, pinch-hit shot off the Padres' Scott Linebrink.*

TODAY'S THOUGHT:

"It was like Frank Sinatra opening for Bob Uecker." *—Pitcher John Trautwein*, on pitching in relief for Roger Clemens

HISTORY:

On this date in 1989 the Giants' Dave Dravecky broke his cancer-ridden arm on the release of a pitch to Tim Raines in a 3-2 win over the Expos. Dravecky, writhing in pain, was carried off the field, dashing his comeback hopes. He retired 19 days later.

BIRTHDAYS:

Tom Kelly, 1950; Scott Brosius, 1966; Oliver Perez, 1981

TRIVIA:

Less than two years after his comeback with the Giants, Dravecky's left arm was amputated. He's written two inspirational books: *Comeback*, published in 1990, and *When You Can't Come Back*, released in 1992.

QUIZ:

Who won four straight Cy Young Awards during the '90s?

ANSWER: *Greg Maddux*, 1992 *to* '95

TODAY'S THOUGHT:

"It doesn't matter what you accomplish in life; the size of your funeral is going to be determined by the weather."
—*Chuck Tanner*, former baseball manager

HISTORY:

On this date in 1920 Cleveland Indians shortstop Ray Chapman suffered a fractured skull when he was hit in the head by pitcher Carl Mays. Chapman died twelve hours later in a New York City hospital. He is the only Major League Baseball player to have been killed in a game.

BIRTHDAYS:

Baby Doll Jacobson, 1890; Gene Woodling, 1922; Rick Reed, 1964; Roger Cedeno, 1974

TRIVIA:

August 16, 1948 marked the death of another baseball player in New York City. Babe Ruth died at the age of 53 from throat cancer.

QUIZ:

On August 16, 1954, *Sports Illustrated* made its debut. What baseball player was featured on the first cover?

ANSWER: *Milwaukee Braves third baseman Ed Mathews*

TODAY'S THOUGHT:

"The difference between hitting .300 and .270 is a hit and a half a week." —*Mark Grace*

HISTORY:

On this date in 1973 New York Mets slugger Willie Mays hit his 660th home run against the Cincinnati Reds. It would be the last of his career.

BIRTHDAYS:

Boog Powell, 1941; Jorge Posada, 1971; Mike Maroth, 1977; Brett Myers, 1980

TRIVIA:

Willie Mays had a vanity license plate that read "SAY HEY." Mays credits sportswriter Jimmy Cannon with creating the nickname.

EXTRA INNING:

"They've taken my playing record off and put my managerial record on."
–*Sparky Anderson*, on why he liked the latest baseball cards

QUIZ:

Who is the only player to win a Triple Crown, the Rookie of the Year Award and be inducted into the Hall of Fame?

ANSWER: *Frank Robinson, who was a unanimous NL Rookie of the Year selection in 1956, won the Triple Crown in 1966 and was inducted into the Hall of Fame in 1982.*

TODAY'S THOUGHT:

"He's a very lucky man. He escapes the dictatorial reign of a ruthless tyrant and ends up working for George Steinbrenner." — *David Letterman*, on Cuban pitcher Orlando Hernandez

HISTORY:

On this date in 1989 George Steinbrenner fired Yankee manager Dallas Green and replaced him with Bucky Dent. This marked the seventeenth time the New York owner changed skippers since taking over in 1973.

BIRTHDAYS:

Burleigh Grimes, 1893; Roberto Clemente, 1934; Bobby Higginson, 1970

TRIVIA:

Joe Torre, who was born in the Bronx, is the only manager in Yankee history who was born in one of New York's five boroughs. He also began his managerial career in Queens, with the Mets in 1977.

QUIZ:

With what team did Joe Torre post his first winning season as a manager? (It wasn't the Mets.)

ANSWER: *The Atlanta Braves - After five losing seasons with New York, Torre moved on to Atlanta and in 1982, his first year there, went 89-73, winning the division.*

TODAY'S THOUGHT:

"Veeck was born into baseball and belongs there Here is an independent thinker, imaginative, uninhibited, innovative He is a promoter at heart but a baseball guy at bottom."

—*Red Smith*

HISTORY:

On this date in 1951 three-foot, seven-inch Eddie Gaedel pinch-hit for the Browns against the Tigers. Wearing the number "1/8," the promotional brainchild of owner Bill Veeck walked on four pitches.

BIRTHDAYS:

Bobby Richardson, 1935; Gary Gaetti, 1958; Woody Williams, 1966; Chris Capuano, 1978

TRIVIA:

Veeck's stunt was not without precedent. In the '30s, Red Sox manager Joe Cronin sent his three-foot, six-inch tall mascot to the plate in an exhibition game.

QUIZ:

Name the last trio of teammates to finish 1-2-3 in a batting race.

ANSWER: *John Olerud (.363), Paul Molitor (.332), and Roberto Alomar (.326) of the Toronto Blue Jays were the top three in batting average in the American League in 1993.*

TODAY'S THOUGHT:

"Every hitter likes fastballs just like everybody likes ice cream. But you don't like it when someone's stuffing it into you by the gallon. That's how you feel when Ryan's throwing balls by you." —*Reggie Jackson*

HISTORY:

On this date in 1974 the California Angels' Nolan Ryan struck out 19 batters but lost, 1-0, in eleven innings to Detroit's Mickey Lolich, who went the distance for the win.

BIRTHDAYS:

Al Lopez, 1908; Mark Langston, 1960; Andy Benes, 1967; Todd Helton, 1973

TRIVIA:

Before 1974 a pitcher had struck out at least 19 opposing batters only three times. In 1974, Nolan Ryan accomplished this twice within eight days, and struck out 19 three times during the season.

QUIZ:

At the end of his career, what pain reliever did Nolan Ryan promote in the 1990's?

ANSWER: *Advil - Ryan actually used the product himself during his final seasons with the Texas Rangers.*

TODAY'S THOUGHT:

"I have only one superstition. I make sure I touch all the bases when I hit a home run." —*Babe Ruth*

HISTORY:

On this date in 1947 the first Little League World Series tournament was held in Williamsport, PA, with the hometown Maynard Midgets winning the inaugural title.

BIRTHDAYS:

John Wetteland, 1966; Craig Counsell, 1970; Ismael Valdez, 1973; Jason Marquis, 1978; B.J. Upton, 1984

TRIVIA:

Speaking of firsts, on this date in 1931, Babe Ruth became the first big leaguer to hit 600 career home runs in a win against the St. Louis Browns.

EXTRA INNING:

"I prefer fast foods." –*Rocky Bridges*, on why he doesn't eat snails

QUIZ:

At what Williamsport ballpark is the Little League World Series annually played?

ANSWER: *Howard J. Lamade Stadium*

TODAY'S THOUGHT:

"Throw strikes. Don't worry about home runs. Babe Ruth is dead." —*Art Fowler*, on the advice he gave as a pitching coach

HISTORY:

On this date in 1989 the Rangers' Nolan Ryan struck out Oakland's Rickey Henderson, becoming the first pitcher with 5,000 career strikeouts. He went on to finish the night with 13 Ks for a total of 5,007, but suffered the loss as Texas fell, 2-0.

BIRTHDAYS:

Ned Hanlon, 1857; Howie Camnitz, 1881; Urban Shocker, 1890; Carl Yastrzemski, 1939; Paul Molitor, 1956; Steve Kline, 1972; Randy Wolf, 1976; Jeff Weaver, 1976

TRIVIA:

Cy Young holds the record for the most games won by a pitcher, 511. However, because of his lengthy career, he also has the most losses, 311.

QUIZ:

In 1986, for the first time in the 20th century, two 300-game winners started against each other. Who were they?

ANSWER: *The Indians' Phil Niekro and the Angels' Don Sutton - The Angels won, but neither Sutton nor Niekro received a decision.*

TODAY'S THOUGHT:

"It wasn't until you hit against him that you knew how fast he really was, until you saw with your own eyes that ball jumping at you."
—*Ted Lyons*, on Bob Feller

HISTORY:

On this date in 1936 seventeen-year old Bob Feller made a spectacular debut for the Cleveland Indians. The young right-hander stuck out 15, including the first eight batters, while allowing only six hits in a 4-1 win over the St. Louis Browns.

BIRTHDAYS:

Mike Boddicker, 1957; Julio Franco, 1961; Mark Bellhorn, 1974

TRIVIA:

Signed by the Indians at age seventeen, Feller tied Dizzy Dean's MLB record of 17 strikeouts in a 1936 game before returning to Iowa at season's end to finish high school.

QUIZ:

Of all the players whose last name begins with "T", which two have the most career home runs? (Hint: You'll be seeing double with this answer.)

ANSWER: *Frank Thomas and Frank Thomas - The latter played for numerous NL clubs in the 1950's and '60s, hitting 286 home runs.*

TODAY'S THOUGHT:

"I'd walk through hell in a gasoline suit to play baseball." —*Pete Rose*

HISTORY:

On this date in 1989 Cincinnati Reds manager Pete Rose, accused of betting on baseball games, was handed a lifetime ban from Major League Baseball by Commissioner A. Bartlett Giamatti.

BIRTHDAYS:

Harry Hooper, 1887; Cal Ripken, Jr., 1960; Tim Salmon, 1968

TRIVIA:

A gambling scandal nearly ruined the careers of Tris Speaker and Ty Cobb in 1926. Both were forced to resign as managers after ex-Tigers pitcher Dutch Leonard claimed Cobb and Speaker bet on at least one game between the Tigers and Indians in 1919. Leonard, however, refused to show up at the hearing for the case, so both men were cleared.

QUIZ:

In what offensive category is Tris Speaker the all-time leader with 792?

ANSWER: *Doubles*

TODAY'S THOUGHT:

"Give him two weeks anywhere on the field and you will have one of the best players at that position in the majors."
—*Jim Frey,* on Ryne Sandberg

HISTORY:

On this date in 1922 the Cubs blew a 25-6 fourth-inning lead but held on to beat the Phillies, 26-23, after Philadelphia left the bases loaded in the ninth. The 49 total runs made the game the highest scoring game in major league history.

BIRTHDAYS:

Rollie Fingers, 1946; Albert Belle, 1966; Doug Glanville, 1970; Gary Mathews, 1974

TRIVIA:

Cub Hall of Famer Ryne Sandberg's folks chose his first name after seeing the name of Yankee pitcher Ryne Duren in a newspaper headline.

QUIZ:

In Ron Guidry's 25-3 season in 1978, all three of his losses came against pitchers named Mike. Who were they?

ANSWER: *Mike Caldwell of the Brewers, Mike Flanagan of the Orioles, and Mike Willis of the Blue Jays*

TODAY'S THOUGHT:

"If the World Series runs seven games, it will be our longest-running show this fall." —*Johnny Carson*, on a bad year for NBC

HISTORY:

On this date in 1939 a Major League Baseball game was televised for the first time. New York station W2XBS broadcast a doubleheader between the Reds and Dodgers at Ebbets Field. Red Barber became the first TV announcer in baseball history.

BIRTHDAYS:

Ricky Bottalico, 1969; Morgan Ensberg, 1975; Alex Sanchez, 1976

TRIVIA:

During the 1995 World Series, NBC's Hannah Storm became the first female sportscaster to host a Fall Classic game and ABC's Lesley Visser became the first female sideline reporter, as coverage of the Series was split between two different networks for the first time.

QUIZ:

Sherry Davis became the first woman public address announcer in MLB history when she was hired by what team in 1993?

ANSWER: *San Francisco Giants*

TODAY'S THOUGHT:

"Sometimes the best deals are the ones you don't make."

—*Bill Veeck*

HISTORY:

On this date in 1982 Rickey Henderson stole third against Milwaukee for his 119th stolen base of the year, breaking the record set by Lou Brock in 1974. Henderson stole four bases on the day to run his total to 122. He'd finished the season with 130.

BIRTHDAYS:

Joe Cunningham, 1931; Buddy Bell, 1951; Jim Thome, 1970; Jose Vidro, 1974

TRIVIA:

The 1964 trade that sent Lou Brock to the Cardinals was one of the most lopsided deals ever. The six-player swap with the Cubs was essentially Brock for pitcher Ernie Broglio. Broglio would play only two more years, winning just three games.

QUIZ:

In another memorable trade, the Cardinals swapped pitchers T.J. Mathews, Eric Ludwick and Blake Stein for whom?

ANSWER: *The A's Mark McGwire, in 1997*

TODAY'S THOUGHT:

"It's a tax write-off." —*Bob Boone*, on getting fined for being ejected

HISTORY:

On this date in 1970 Tigers pitcher Denny McLain was suspended seven days for an incident in which he doused two Detroit writers with buckets of ice water. He was also suspended that year for his involvement in a book-making operation and waving a gun in a restaurant.

BIRTHDAYS:

Charlie Grimm, 1898; Lou Piniella, 1943; Mike Torrez, 1946; Ron Guidry, 1950; Jay Witasick, 1972

TRIVIA:

In 1981 Seattle manager Maury Wills was suspended two games and fined $500 for asking the Kingdome's grounds crew to enlarge the batter's box by a foot before a game against Oakland. A's manager Billy Martin noticed the change before the game.

QUIZ:

Name the winning and losing pitchers in the 1978 American League playoff game between Boston and New York.

ANSWER: *The Yankees' Ron Guidry got the win, while Mike Torrez suffered the loss.*

TODAY'S THOUGHT:

"Hitting is timing. Pitching is upsetting timing." —*Warren Spahn*

HISTORY:

On this date in 2002 the Cubs' Mark Bellhorn became the first National Leaguer to hit a home run from both sides of the plate in the same inning. Bellhorn racked up five RBIs on his two shots in the Cubs' 10-run fourth inning against the Brewers.

BIRTHDAYS:

Aaron Rowand, 1977; Roy Oswalt, 1977

TRIVIA:

Yankee Tony Lazzeri was the first major leaguer to hit two grand slams in a game. He did it on May 24, 1936, in a 25-2 rout of the Philadelphia A's.

QUIZ:

Who's the only leadoff hitter in the modern era of baseball to lead his team in both homers and RBI's in a season?

ANSWER: *Bobby Bonds, in 1973 led the San Francisco Giants with 39 dingers and 96 RBI's.*

TODAY'S THOUGHT:

"You've got to remember - I'm 73." —*Ty Cobb*, on why he felt he could hit only .300 against modern pitching

HISTORY:

On this date in 1905 eighteen-year-old Detroit rookie Ty Cobb made his major league debut. His first hit, a two-run double, came off New York Highlanders pitcher Jack Chesbro in a 5-3 Tigers victory.

BIRTHDAYS:

Bing Miller, 1894; Kiki Cuyler, 1898; Ted Williams, 1918; Tug McGraw, 1944; Marlon Byrd, 1977; Cliff Lee, 1978

TRIVIA:

Exactly one year later, the New York Highlanders began a curious winning streak in which they would sweep five straight doubleheaders in a six-day period. After a few more consecutive wins, the Highlanders had put together a 15-game win streak in eleven days.

QUIZ:

Only one major leaguer has won a batting title in three different decades. Who?

ANSWER: *George Brett, in 1976, 1980, and 1990*

TODAY'S THOUGHT:

"My wife wanted a big diamond." —*Mookie Wilson*, on why he was getting married in a baseball stadium

HISTORY:

On this date in 1990 Ken Griffey, Sr. and Ken Griffey, Jr. became the first father-son duo in baseball history to play together when they took the outfield for the Seattle Mariners. Each Griffey went 1-for-4 in Seattle's win over the Royals.

BIRTHDAYS:

Eddie Plank, 1875; Ray Dandridge, 1913; Frank Robinson, 1935; Hideo Nomo, 1968; Gabe Kapler, 1975

TRIVIA:

After being in the majors for just one month, the younger Griffey had a chocolate candy bar named after him. Ironically, because Griffey, Jr., is allergic to chocolate, he was never able to sample his own product.

QUIZ:

Babe Ruth hit his "called" shot in the 1932 World Series against what Cubs pitcher?

ANSWER: *Charlie Root*

TODAY'S THOUGHT:

"Some right fielders have rifles for arms, but he had a howitzer."
—*Tim McCarver*, on Roberto Clemente

HISTORY:

On this date in 1971 the Pittsburgh Pirates started what is believed to be the first all-black team in MLB history. The lineup: Rennie Stennett, 2B; Gene Clines, CF; Roberto Clemente, RF; Willie Stargell, LF; Manny Sanguillen, C; Dave Cash, 3B; Al Oliver, 1B; Jackie Hernandez, SS; and Dock Ellis, P. They beat the Phillies, 10-7.

BIRTHDAYS:

Jim O'Rourke, 1850; Rico Carty, 1939

TRIVIA:

Only once in the team's history has a Pirates manager won more than 100 games in the regular season. Fred Clarke did it in 1902 with a 103-36 record, and again in 1909, with a mark of 110-42.

QUIZ:

Willie Stargell was selected NL co-MVP in 1979 along with what other player?

ANSWER: *Keith Hernandez*

TODAY'S THOUGHT:

"I'd rather be lucky than good." —*Lefty Gomez*

HISTORY:

On this date in 1990 Toronto's Dave Stieb recorded his first no-hitter against Cleveland, 3-0. Four times before, Stieb had entered the ninth-inning of a game with a no-hitter, and all four times the opposing teams had broken them up - three times with two outs.

BIRTHDAYS:

Al Spalding, 1850; Rich Aurilia, 1971

TRIVIA:

In the first start of his major league career, St. Louis Browns pitcher Alva Lee "Bobo" Holloman no-hit the Philadelphia Athletics. Holloman would pitch in just twenty-one more games in his one-year stint in the majors, finishing with a career record of 3-7.

QUIZ:

What major league stadium never saw a no-hitter in its more than 60 years of existence?

ANSWER: *Pittsburgh's Forbes Field*

TODAY'S THOUGHT:

"Nolan Ryan is pitching much better now that he has his curve ball straightened out." —*Joe Garagiola*

HISTORY:

On this date in 1990 Chicago White Sox reliever Bobby Thigpen earned his 47th save of the season and a place in major league history. Thigpen, who finished the year with 57 saves, broke Dave Righetti's record of 46 set in 1986.

BIRTHDAYS:

Eddie Stanky, 1916; Luis Gonzalez, 1967

TRIVIA:

The Rolaids Relief Award, which was first given out in 1976, is the only official Major League Baseball award that is commercially sponsored.

QUIZ:

What pitcher holds the major league record for the most consecutive saves?

ANSWER: *Eric Gagne, with 84*

TODAY'S THOUGHT:

"Are you a natural left-hander?" —A reporter, to Jim Abbott , who was born without a right hand

HISTORY:

On this date in 1993 Jim Abbott no-hit the Cleveland Indians, 4-0, at Yankee Stadium. It was one of three no-hitters pitched in the majors that year.

BIRTHDAYS:

Frank White, 1950; Mike Piazza, 1968

TRIVIA:

Mordecai "Three Finger" Brown, a six-time 20-game winner with the Chicago Cubs in the early 1900's, lost parts of his fingers in a farm machinery accident. He was actually aided in his pitching by his mangled hand, which allowed him to throw an early version of the split-finger fastball.

EXTRA INNING:

"I tried real hard not to get any muscles so I wouldn't hurt them."
–*Dan Quisenberry*, on his off-season preparation

QUIZ:

Where did Jim Abbott play his college ball?

ANSWER: *Abbott pitched for the Michigan Wolverines.*

TODAY'S THOUGHT:

"Most pitchers are too smart to manage." —*Jim Palmer*

HISTORY:

On this date in 1918 Game One of the World Series was played a month early because of World War I. The Red Sox defeated the Cubs, 1-0, behind Babe Ruth's complete game shutout. The first three games of the Series were moved to the South Side, at Comiskey Park, for more seating.

BIRTHDAYS:

Nap Lajoie, 1874; Bill Mazeroski, 1936

TRIVIA:

Sources say the national anthem was sung for the first time at a professional sporting event at that game. It was performed during the seventh inning stretch.

QUIZ:

What two teams are tied for the most World Series titles without a Series loss?

ANSWER: *The Florida Marlins and Toronto Blue Jays, with two each, have never lost a World Series.*

TODAY'S THOUGHT:

"We consider ourselves the luckiest fans on the face of the earth." —*Sign seen at Oriole Park at Camden Yards*

HISTORY:

On this date in 1995 Cal Ripken, Jr., of the Baltimore Orioles played in his 2,131st consecutive game, breaking Lou Gehrig's record. When the game became official after the top of the 5th inning, Ripken received a 22-minute standing ovation from Baltimore fans.

BIRTHDAYS:

Oyster Burns, 1864; Red Faber, 1888; Vince DiMaggio, 1912; Derrek Lee, 1975; Mark Teahan, 1981

TRIVIA:

The next season Ripken would break the world record of 2,215 consecutive games played, held by Sachio Kinugasa, the Ironman of Japanese baseball. As a third baseman for the Hiroshima Carp, Kinugasa's streak began in 1970 and lasted until he retired seventeen years later.

QUIZ:

What team was the opponent in Ripken's record-setting game?

ANSWER: *The California Angels - The Orioles won the game, 4-2. Ripken homered in the victory.*

TODAY'S THOUGHT:

"I had slumps that lasted into the winter." —*Bob Uecker*

HISTORY:

On this date in 1993 Mark Whiten of the St. Louis Cardinals tied three major league records in a doubleheader against Cincinnati. Whiten had four homers and 12 runs-batted-in in the nightcap, totaling 13 RBIs for the day.

BIRTHDAYS:

Hooks Wiltse, 1879; Curt Davis, 1903; Jason Isringhausen, 1972; Mark Prior, 1980

TRIVIA:

In 1905 Honus Wagner became the first player to have his autograph branded into a Louisville Slugger baseball bat.

EXTRA INNING:

"I felt like I collided with a Mercedes Benzinger." –*Dennis Lamp*, on running into teammate Todd Benzinger

QUIZ:

Who is the first man to homer in his first two major league at-bats?

ANSWER: *Bob Nieman of the St. Louis Browns, in 1951*

TODAY'S THOUGHT:

"There's only one thing bigger than me, and that's my ego."
—*Dave Parker*

HISTORY:

On this date in 1998 the Cardinals' Mark McGwire hit his 62nd home run of the season, beating the Cubs' Sammy Sosa in the race to break Roger Maris' mark of 61. Sosa finished the year with 66 home runs and McGwire with 70.

BIRTHDAYS:

Ken Forsch, 1946; Gil Meche, 1978

TRIVIA:

McGwire's Cardinals faced off against Sosa's Cubs in St. Louis when McGwire made history. Chicago pitcher Steve Trachsel went into the record books as the man who gave up number 62.

EXTRA INNING:

"You feel like a starting pitcher. Afterwards you need three days' rest."
–*Joe Garagiola*, on having dinner with Tommy Lasorda

QUIZ:

What pitcher did Sammy Sosa hit his 62nd home run off in 1998?

ANSWER: *Milwaukee Brewers' reliever Eric Plunk*

TODAY'S THOUGHT:

"Show me the guy who can't pitch inside and I'll show you a loser." —*Sandy Koufax*

HISTORY:

On this date in 1965 Bob Hendley of the Cubs tossed a one-hitter against the Dodgers and lost, 1-0. Sandy Koufax got the decision on the strength of his fourth career no-hitter and his first perfect game.

BIRTHDAYS:

Frank Chance, 1877; Frankie Frisch, 1898; Waite Hoyt, 1899; Todd Zeile, 1965; Mike Hampton, 1972; Kaz Ishii, 1973

TRIVIA:

Five days later Hendley and Koufax faced off again. This time Hendley pitched a four-hitter and beat Koufax and the Dodgers, 2-1.

EXTRA INNING:

"People think we make $3 million and $ 4 million a year. They don't realize that most of us only make $500,000." –*Pete Incaviglia*

QUIZ:

What pitcher had a record of 18-1 in 1959?

ANSWER: *Roy Face, of the Pittsburgh Pirates*

TODAY'S THOUGHT:

"Bruce Benedict is so slow, he'd finish third in a race with a pregnant woman." —*Tommy Lasorda*

HISTORY:

On this date in 1974 Lou Brock tied Maury Wills' single-season stolen base mark in the first inning, then broke it in the seventh with his 105th steal of the year. Brock ended the season with 118 stolen bases, but would be passed in 1982 by Rickey Henderson.

BIRTHDAYS:

George Kelly, 1895; Ted Kluszewski, 1924; Roger Maris, 1934; Randy Johnson, 1963; Danys Baez, 1977

TRIVIA:

The only two players to lead off both games of a doubleheader with a home run are Harry Hooper and Rickey Henderson. Hooper did it for the Red Sox in 1913 against Washington, eighty years before the A's Henderson hit two in a twin bill against the Indians.

QUIZ:

Three players in Major League Baseball history have stolen bases in four different decades. Rickey Henderson is one. Name the other two.

ANSWER: *Ted Williams and Tim Raines*

TODAY'S THOUGHT:

"There is an old saying, 'money can't buy happiness.' If it could, I would buy myself four hits every game." —*Pete Rose*

HISTORY:

On this date in 1985 Cincinnati's Pete Rose became Major League Baseball's all-time hits leader surpassing Ty Cobb's 4,191 in a Reds' 2–0 win over San Diego. When Rose retired, he left a new mark of 4,256 hits.

BIRTHDAYS:

Don Slaught, 1958; Ellis Burks, 1964

TRIVIA:

Pete Rose holds the modern record for the most consecutive game-hitting streaks of 20 or more games with seven.

EXTRA INNING:

"What we could use is a couple of shutouts, but I don't know if that would be good enough to win." –*Whitey Herzog*, on a weak-hitting St. Louis Cardinals team

QUIZ:

Three players have been named World Series MVP more than once. Name them.

ANSWER: *Sandy Koufax in 1963 and 1965; Bob Gibson in 1964 and 1967; Reggie Jackson in 1973 and 1977*

TODAY'S THOUGHT:

"Baseball is supposed to be a non-contact sport, but our hitters seem to be taking that literally."
—*Larry Doughty*, former Pirates GM

HISTORY:

On this date in 1962 Washington's Tom Cheney, after finishing the first nine innings with "just" 13 Ks, went on to strike out a record 21 batters in a 16-inning, 2-1 win at Baltimore.

BIRTHDAYS:

Spud Chandler, 1907; Charlie Keller, 1916; Andy Seminick, 1920; Mickey Lolich, 1940; Luis Castillo, 1975; Sean Burroughs, 1980

TRIVIA:

Another pitching ace making history on this day was the Mets' Dwight Gooden, who in 1984 struck out 16 Pirates in a 2-0 shutout. In doing so, Gooden set a rookie major league strikeout record with 251. He would finish the season with 276 Ks.

QUIZ:

In 2004, what hitter broke Bobby Bonds' single-season strikeout record by being fanned 195 times?

ANSWER: *Adam Dunn, of the Cincinnati Reds*

TODAY'S THOUGHT:

"Managing is getting paid for home runs someone else hits."
—*Casey Stengel*

HISTORY:

On this date in 1965 and 1971 a pair of Hall of Famers hit their 500th career home runs. In 1965, the Giants' Willie Mays joined the 500 Club by homering against the Astros, while six years later the Orioles' Frank Robinson hit numbers 499 and 500 in a doubleheader against the Tigers.

BIRTHDAYS:

Rick Wise, 1945; Bernie Williams, 1968; Denny Neagle, 1968; Wade Miller, 1976

TRIVIA:

The uniform number of baseball comedian Max Patkin was? (That was a statement.)

QUIZ:

True or False? Outfielders Mickey Mantle and Willie Mays both played shortstop in the majors.

ANSWER: *True - Mantle played short seven times, while Mays was pencilled in there twice.*

September 14

TODAY'S THOUGHT:

"Baseball is a game where a curve is an optical illusion, a screwball can be a pitch or a person, stealing is legal and you can spit anywhere you like except in the umpire's eye or on the ball." —*Jim Murray*

HISTORY:

On this date in 1968 Detroit Tigers ace Denny McLain won his thirtieth game of the season, 5-4, over the A's. He would finish the year with a 31-6 mark, becoming the first and last pitcher to win 30 games since Dizzy Dean in 1934.

BIRTHDAYS:

Kid Nichols, 1869; David Bell, 1972; Chad Bradford, 1974

TRIVIA:

In 2003, McLain, who's had many brushes with the law, began working as a clerk at a 7-Eleven in Michigan as part of an eight-year federal prison sentence for embezzlement. He was convicted after $3 million went missing from his company's pension fund in 1997.

QUIZ:

Five Cy Young winners are convicted felons. Denny McLain is one. Name the other four.

ANSWER: *Lamarr Hoyt, Dwight Gooden, Vida Blue, and Ferguson Jenkins*

TODAY'S THOUGHT:

"When Steve Carlton and I die, we are going to be buried in the same cemetery, sixty feet, six inches apart."
—*Tim McCarver*, Lefty's personal batterymate

HISTORY:

On this date in 1969 Steve Carlton became the first pitcher in the twentieth century to strike out 19 batters in a nine-inning game - but lost anyway. Carlton fanned everyone in the Mets lineup at least once, but Ron Swoboda hit two homers to defeat the Cardinals, 4-3.

BIRTHDAY:

Gaylord Perry, 1938

TRIVIA:

Only one Hall of Fame player has worn the number 13 – Roberto Clemente, in 1955, his rookie year with the Pirates. The following year, and for the rest of his career, he wore number 21. (Hall of Famer Burleigh Grimes wore #13 as a manager.)

QUIZ:

Name the only player to win two batting titles for the Chicago Cubs.

ANSWER: *Bill Madlock - While he spent only three seasons in Chicago, he won back- to-back batting titles with the team in 1975 and 1976.*

TODAY'S THOUGHT:

"How can a guy win a game if you don't give him any runs?"
—*Bo Belinsky*, after losing a game, 15-0

HISTORY:

On this date in 1975 Rennie Stennett led the Pirates to a 22-0 win over the Cubs, the most lopsided shutout in modern major league history. Stennett sparked the club by going seven for seven, tying a record set by Wilbert Robinson in 1892.

BIRTHDAYS:

Robin Yount, 1955; Orel Hershiser, 1958; Mel Hall, 1960; Mickey Tettleton, 1960; Tim Raines, 1959; Paul Shuey, 1970

TRIVIA:

In 2004, the Cleveland Indians equalled the Pirates' tremendous performance by scoring 22 runs and shutting out the New York Yankees. In the game, Omar Vizquel nearly matched Stennett's record by getting six hits in seven at-bats.

QUIZ:

After game seven of the 1997 World Series, what teammate did Omar Vizquel call a "choker" and blame for the Indians' loss to the Marlins?

ANSWER: *Pitcher Jose Mesa, who vowed to hit Vizquel every time he faced him*

TODAY'S THOUGHT:

"Fans don't boo nobodies." —*Reggie Jackson*

HISTORY:

On this date in 1984 on the seventeenth anniversary of his first major league home run, Reggie Jackson connected off Kansas City's Bud Black for his 500th career round-tripper. Jackson accounted for the lone run in a 10-1 Angels' loss to the Royals.

BIRTHDAYS:

Orlando Cepeda, 1937; John Franco, 1960; Danny Haren, 1980

TRIVIA:

Bob Watson scored Major League Baseball's one-millionth run in 1975.

EXTRA INNING:

"The best qualification a coach can have is being the manager's drinking buddy." –*Jim Bouton*

QUIZ:

During the Seattle Pilots' only season in the American League, what pitcher led the team in both wins and losses?

ANSWER: *Gene Brabender went 13 and 14 with the club in 1969.*

TODAY'S THOUGHT:

"The only difference between Candlestick and San Quentin is that at Candlestick they let you go home at night." —*Jim Wohlford*

HISTORY:

On this date in 1968 Cardinals pitcher Ray Washburn no-hit the Giants at Candlestick Park, 2-0. Less than 24 hours earlier, Gaylord Perry of the Giants no-hit St. Louis, 1-0. As a result, history was made with two consecutive no-hitters being thrown in the same park.

BIRTHDAYS:

George Uhle, 1898; Ryne Sandberg, 1959; Jody Gerut, 1977

TRIVIA:

A.J. Burnett holds the record for the most walks allowed in a nine-inning no-hitter, when the Florida hurler walked nine in a 3-0 victory over San Diego in 2001. Burnett also hit Padre Damian Jackson in the third inning.

QUIZ:

George "Duffy" Lewis was to Babe Ruth what Mike Lum was to Hank Aaron. What?

ANSWER: *Their only pinch-hitters*

TODAY'S THOUGHT:

"Baseball is the only sport I know that when you're on offense, the other team controls the ball." —*Ken Harrelson*, White Sox general manager

HISTORY:

On this date in 1998 Mariners shortstop Alex Rodriguez became the first infielder in MLB history to have 40 home runs and 40 steals in one season. Rodriguez hit his fortieth round-tripper of the year off the Angels' Jack McDowell.

BIRTHDAYS:

Duke Snider, 1926; Bob Turley, 1930; Joe Morgan, 1943; Jim Abbott, 1967; Nick Johnson, 1978

TRIVIA:

In the 2005 Home Run Derby, the Phillies' Bobby Abreu hit a contest record 24 home runs in the first round. His final three-round total of 41 more than doubled that of runner-up Ivan Rodriguez.

QUIZ:

Who was the only player to be there, in uniform, when Roger Maris hit his 61st homer and Hank Aaron clouted number 715?

ANSWER: *Al Downing*

TODAY'S THOUGHT:

"Your body is just like a bar of soap. It gradually wears down from repeated use." —*Richie Allen*

HISTORY:

On this date in 1998 Cal Ripken, Jr., took himself out of the starting lineup and did not play in the Baltimore Orioles' loss to the New York Yankees, ending his consecutive-game streak at 2,632 games. Ripken's streak had lasted 16 years.

BIRTHDAYS:

Chuck Dressen, 1898; Jason Bay, 1978

TRIVIA:

Ripken's record-breaking night against the Angels in 1995 was the first game outside of Washington ever attended by both a president (Bill Clinton) and vice president (Al Gore).

QUIZ:

Who is the only major league player to have two streaks of at least 650 consecutive games played?

ANSWER: *Pete Rose - During his career, "Charlie Hustle" had separate streaks of 678 (from 1973-78) and 745 (1978-83) games played in a row.*

TODAY'S THOUGHT:

"I ain't what I used to be, but who the hell is?" —*Dizzy Dean*

HISTORY:

On this date in 1934 the St. Louis Cardinals' Dean brothers staged a double feature. Dizzy pitched a three-hit shutout in the opener of a doubleheader, beating the Dodgers, 13-0. His brother, Paul, pitched a 3-0 no-hitter in the nightcap.

BIRTHDAYS:

Sam McDowell, 1942; Cecil Fielder, 1963; Scott Spiezio, 1972; Doug Davis, 1975

TRIVIA:

Dizzy, whose real name is Jay Hanna Dean, was the winning pitcher in the National League's first All-Star Game victory in 1936.

QUIZ:

Who are the only brothers to finish first and second in a major league batting race?

ANSWER: *Matty and Felipe Alou - Matty hit .342 in 1966, while Felipe hit .327.*

TODAY'S THOUGHT:

"All of his saves have come during relief appearances."
—*Ralph Kiner*, on Steve Bedrosian

HISTORY:

On this date in 1911 the 22-year pitching career of Cy Young ended with a 1-0 victory over Pittsburgh. Both Young's 511 career wins and 749 complete games remain unchallenged as major league records.

BIRTHDAYS:

Hooks Dauss, 1889; Bob Lemon, 1920; Tommy Lasorda, 1927; Larry Dierker, 1946; Wally Backman, 1959; Vince Coleman, 1961; Mike Matheny, 1970

TRIVIA:

Cy Young's real name was Denton True Young.

QUIZ:

The pitcher who started the first game ever for the Florida Marlins is also the only hurler in Major League Baseball history with at least 375 starts and 375 relief appearances. Who is he?

ANSWER: *Charlie Hough*

TODAY'S THOUGHT:

"I don't see pitches down the middle anymore - not even in batting practice." —*Hank Aaron*

HISTORY:

On this date in 1908 baseball's most famous boneheaded play occurred when the Giants' Fred Merkle failed to touch second base after an apparent game-winning hit by teammate Al Bridwell. The lapse in judgement caused New York to lose the game, and ultimately the pennant, to the Chicago Cubs.

BIRTHDAY:

Jeff Cirillo, 1969

TRIVIA:

The Cubs' second baseman that tagged the bag, forcing out Merkle, was Johnny Evers of Tinker-to-Evers- to-Chance fame.

QUIZ:

Who followed Bart Giamatti as Commissioner of Baseball after Giamatti's untimely death in 1989?

ANSWER: *Fay Vincent*

TODAY'S THOUGHT:

"Hitting is better than sex." —*Reggie Jackson*

HISTORY:

On this date in 1940 Boston's Jimmie Foxx became just the second major leaguer to hit 500 career home runs in a 16-8 victory over Philadelphia. Foxx would finish with 534 total homers.

BIRTHDAYS:

Dixie Walker, 1910; Rafael Palmeiro, 1964; Kevin Millar, 1971; Ben Broussard, 1976

TRIVIA:

Hall of Fame pitchers Bob Gibson and Ferguson Jenkins both played for the Harlem Globetrotters.

QUIZ:

Of all the players who spent their entire careers with one team, who has the most home runs?

ANSWER: *Mike Schmidt, who hit 548 homers during his career with the Phillies*

TODAY'S THOUGHT:

"It got so that I could nip the frosting off a cake with my fastball."
—*Satchel Paige*

HISTORY:

On this date in 1965 in a publicity stunt, fifty-nine year-old Satchel Paige pitched three scoreless innings of one-hit ball for the Kansas City Athletics in a 5-2 victory over the Red Sox. Paige last pitched in the big leagues in 1953.

BIRTHDAYS:

Phil Rizzuto, 1917; Tony Womack, 1969; David Weathers, 1969; Joel Pineiro, 1978; Rocco Baldelli, 1981

TRIVIA:

Officially opened in 1939, the Baseball Hall of Fame is the first such institution devoted to a sport.

QUIZ:

Who's the only big leaguer to have worn his birthday on his back?

ANSWER: *Carlos May - His number was 17 and his last name, which appeared above the number, combined with it to form his birth date.*

TODAY'S THOUGHT:

"Son, we'd like to keep you around this season, but we're going to try to win a pennant."
—*Casey Stengel*, on cutting Aubrey Gatewood

HISTORY:

On this date in 1954 the Cleveland Indians closed the regular season with 111 victories, an American League record. They put an end to the Yankees' five consecutive pennants and titles streak, but Cleveland would be swept by the Giants in the World Series.

BIRTHDAY:

Bobby Shantz, 1925

TRIVIA:

The Indians won the World Series in 1948, and after they were eliminated from playoff contention the following season, owner Bill Veeck held a mock funeral at Municipal Stadium to bury the '48 pennant.

QUIZ:

What player has won the most World Series titles, with ten?

ANSWER: *The Yankees' Yogi Berra, who played in fourteen Fall Classics, more than anyone else*

TODAY'S THOUGHT:

"Pete Rose is the most likeable arrogant person I have ever met." —*Mike Schmidt*

HISTORY:

On this date in 1963 the Houston Colt .45s started the first and only all-rookie lineup in MLB history against the Mets. Despite future stars like Joe Morgan and Rusty Staub, the freshman team, with an average age of 19 years old, lost to New York, 10-3.

BIRTHDAYS:

Johnny Pesky, 1919; Mike Schmidt, 1949; Vincente Padilla, 1977; Jon Garland, 1979

TRIVIA:

Houston's right fielder that day was a little-known player named Aaron Pointer. His better-known sisters had a few hits of their own - performing as the Pointer Sisters.

QUIZ:

Who stole the most bases in the 1990s?

ANSWER: *Otis Nixon, who stole 478 bases*

TODAY'S THOUGHT:

"If I'm going to be a .400 hitter I want to have more than my toenails on the line." —*Ted Williams*

HISTORY:

On this date in 1941 Ted Williams had four hits in five at-bats in the first game of a doubleheader in Philadelphia to bring his average to .404. He went 2 for 3 in game two to finish the season with a .406 batting average.

BIRTHDAYS:

Jack Fournier, 1889; Todd Worrell, 1959; Ryan Zimmerman, 1984

TRIVIA:

Williams entered the last day of the season hitting .39955, which rounded off would make him a .400 hitter. Since the doubleheader against Philadelphia was meaningless for Boston, manager Joe Cronin offered Williams a chance to sit. Clearly, the Splendid Splinter had other ideas.

QUIZ:

What two players reached the 3,000 hit plateau on consecutive days in 1999?

ANSWER: *Tony Gwynn reached the mark on August 6th, and Wade Boggs did it the next day.*

TODAY'S THOUGHT:

"Let's play two!" —*Ernie Banks*

HISTORY:

On this date in 1987 Yankees first baseman Don Mattingly hit a record sixth grand slam of the season, off Boston's Bruce Hurst in a 6–0 Yankees win. He broke the old mark shared by Ernie Banks and Jim Gentile.

BIRTHDAYS:

Rob Deer, 1960; Jake Westbrook, 1977

TRIVIA:

When Cubs manager Whitey Lockman was ejected from a 1973 game, coach Ernie Banks filled in for the last couple of innings of a 3-2 win over the Padres. Thus, Mr. Cub was technically baseball's first black manager, predating Frank Robinson by nearly two years.

QUIZ:

Name the five players named Williams who have more than 200 home runs.

ANSWER: *Ted, Billy, Matt, Cy and Bernie*

TODAY'S THOUGHT:

"You can never have too much talent. Even the 1927 Yankees didn't win every year." —*Buzzie Bavasi*

HISTORY:

On this date in 1927 Babe Ruth became the first player to hit 60 home runs in one year, blasting a shot off Washington's Tom Zachary. New York defeated the Senators, 4-2, at Yankee Stadium.

BIRTHDAYS:

Gabby Street, 1882; Robin Roberts, 1926; Johnny Podres, 1932; Dave Magadan, 1962; Jose Lima, 1972; Jeremy Giambi, 1974

TRIVIA:

Washington's great pitcher, Walter Johnson, holds the career record for hit batsmen - 206.

EXTRA INNING:

"I once scouted a pitcher who was so bad that when he came into a game the grounds crew dragged the warning-track." –Chicago White Sox scout *Fred Smith*

QUIZ:

Who holds the record for the most home runs hit in Yankee Stadium?

ANSWER: *Mickey Mantle*, 266

TODAY'S THOUGHT:

"As a ballplayer, I would be delighted to do it again. As an individual, I doubt if I could possibly go through it again."
—*Roger Maris*

HISTORY:

On this date in 1961 Roger Maris broke the record many thought impossible to break, hitting his sixty-first home run in the final game of the season. His solo shot off Tracy Stallard gave the Yankees a 1-0 win over Boston and snapped the mark set thirty-four years earlier by Babe Ruth.

BIRTHDAYS:

Rod Carew, 1945; Mark McGwire, 1963; Roberto Kelly, 1964

TRIVIA:

Maris' record-breaking home run ball was caught by 19 year-old New York City truck driver Sal Durante. Durante presented the ball to Maris after the game.

QUIZ:

Who was the only player to hit four home runs in a game and three triples in another?

ANSWER: *Willie Mays*

TODAY'S THOUGHT:

"Gibson's the luckiest pitcher I've ever seen because he always picks the night to pitch when the other team doesn't score any runs." —*Tim McCarver*, on Bob Gibson

HISTORY:

On this date in 1968 Bob Gibson got St. Louis off to a good start in the first game of the World Series, striking out seventeen Detroit batters in a 4-0 Cardinals win. Gibson broke the record set by Sandy Koufax.

BIRTHDAYS:

Maury Wills, 1932; Earl Wilson, 1934; Eddie Guardado, 1970; Scott Schoeneweis, 1973

TRIVIA:

Exactly five years earlier, LA's Sandy Koufax broke Carl Erskine's World Series strikeout record by fanning fifteen Yankees in a 5-2 win. Erskine set his record exactly ten years before that, striking out fourteen Yankees in a 3-2 Brooklyn victory.

QUIZ:

In 1967, at the age of nineteen, I became the youngest player to pitch in the World Series. Who am I?

ANSWER: *Ken Brett of the Boston Red Sox*

TODAY'S THOUGHT:

"Brooklyn is all right, but if you're not with the Giants, you might as well be in Albany."
—*Bill Dahlen*, Giants shortstop, in 1904

HISTORY:

On this date in 1951 Bobby Thomson hit the "shot heard 'round the world." His three-run homer in the ninth inning off Brooklyn's Ralph Branca in game three of the National League playoff gave the New York Giants a 5-4 win - and the pennant.

BIRTHDAYS:

Fred Clarke, 1872; Dave Winfield, 1951; Dennis Eckersley, 1954

TRIVIA:

A home run by Thomson was also the margin of victory in the first playoff game that year. The pitcher? Ralph Branca.

EXTRA INNING:

"But I'm only thirty-two in the Dominican Republic." -42-year-old Florida outfielder *Tim Raines*, on his age

QUIZ:

What slugger has hit the most home runs in a single major league park - and where?

ANSWER: *Mel Ott of the New York Giants, 323 in the Polo Grounds*

TODAY'S THOUGHT:

"You observe a lot by just watching." —*Yogi Berra*

HISTORY:

On this date in 1955 after decades of frustration, the Brooklyn Dodgers won their first World Series. Johnny Podres pitched eight shutout innings and received a major defensive assist from leftfielder Sandy Amoros in the 2-0 Game Seven win over the New York Yankees.

BIRTHDAYS:

Jimy Williams, 1943; Tony LaRussa, 1944

TRIVIA:

After winning pennants in 1941, '47, '49, '52, and '53, the Dodgers lost in all five World Series to the Yankees. The trend of falling just short of a championship inspired the phrase, "Wait 'til next year!," and became the unofficial Dodger slogan.

QUIZ:

Since 1920, what is the only decade the Yankees failed to win a World Series?

ANSWER: *The 1980s*

TODAY'S THOUGHT:

"The World Series is American sports' annual ticket to a romantic yesterday, when we were all young and surely going to be in the big leagues someday." —*Ray Fitzgerald, The Sporting News*

HISTORY:

On this date in 1953 the Yankees set a new mark winning their fifth straight World Series title. Billy Martin's record-setting twelfth hit of the Series in the bottom of the ninth gave New York a 4-3 win over the Dodgers in the sixth and final game of the Fall Classic.

BIRTHDAY:

Rey Sanchez, 1967

TRIVIA:

Vin Scully and Mel Allen were teamed to broadcast the 1953 World Series on NBC. Scully was twenty-five years-old, the youngest sportscaster ever for the Fall Classic.

QUIZ:

Name the only player in the Baseball Hall of Fame whose last name begins with the letter "I".

ANSWER: *Monte Irvin*

TODAY'S THOUGHT:

"There's a soft liner, which is caught by the second baseman. And the ball game is over! For this inning." —*Jerry Coleman*

HISTORY:

On this date in 1963 the LA Dodgers completed their World Series sweep of the New York Yankees. Sandy Koufax led the way with his second win of the Series, a 2-1 victory at Dodger Stadium.

BIRTHDAYS:

Ruben Sierra, 1965; Darren Oliver, 1970

TRIVIA:

The 1947 World Series, in which the Yankees beat the Dodgers in seven games, was the first to be telecast. While coverage was limited to the New York City area, an estimated 3.9 million people watched it.

EXTRA INNING:

"When I am right, no one remembers. When I am wrong, no one forgets."
–*Doug Harvey*, umpire

QUIZ:

The New York Yankees, with twenty-six titles, obviously have won the most World Series Championships. What team is a distant second?

ANSWER: *The St. Louis Cardinals, with nine*

TODAY'S THOUGHT:

"Sometimes I surprise my own damn self." —*Barry Bonds*

HISTORY:

On this date in 2001 Barry Bonds extended his single-season home run record total to seventy-three when he smacked a pitch off Dodgers hurler Dennis Springer in a 2-1 Giants' win.

BIRTHDAYS:

Chuck Klein, 1904; Jose Cardenal, 1943

TRIVIA:

That year Bonds also set the single-season record for slugging percentage with .863, surpassing Babe Ruth's eighty-one year-old mark.

EXTRA INNING:

"I owe it all to my parents." –San Francisco Giants rookie pitcher *David Aardsma*, on ending Hank Aaron's fifty-year reign atop the alphabetical list of big leaguers

QUIZ:

A baseball first occurred in 1960 when Detroit traded Jimmie Dykes to Cleveland for Joe Gordon. What was unique about it?

ANSWER: *They were managers.*

TODAY'S THOUGHT:

"If Nolan Ryan had done it, if Sandy Koufax had done it, if Don Drysdale had done it, I would have nodded and said, 'Well, it could happen.' But Don Larsen?" —*Bob Sheppard*, Yankees public-address announcer

HISTORY:

On this date in 1956 Yankees pitcher Don Larsen, who couldn't get past the second inning of his first start against Brooklyn, hurled the only perfect game in World Series history, a 2-0 Game Five victory. Larsen threw only 97 pitches.

BIRTHDAYS:

Wally Moses, 1910; Danny Murtaugh, 1917; Mike Morgan, 1959

TRIVIA:

Brooklyn shortstop Pee Wee Reese was the only batter to even reach ball three against Larsen. Reese was called out on strikes in the first inning.

EXTRA INNING:

"The Cubs went over 2.1 million on Sunday. But enough about games behind." –*Steve Rosenbloom* of the *Chicago Tribune*

QUIZ:

Who was the losing pitcher in Larsen's perfect game and who made the last out?

ANSWER: *Sal Maglie and Dale Mitchell*

TODAY'S THOUGHT:

"You gotta lose 'em sometime. When you do, lose 'em right."
—*Casey Stengel*

HISTORY:

On this date in 2005 the Astros defeated the Braves in the longest postseason game in MLB history. A home run by Chris Burke in the bottom of the eighteenth inning gave Houston a 7-6 Game Four win, sending them into the NL Championship Series.

BIRTHDAYS:

Rube Marquard, 1889; Joe Sewell, 1898; Brian Downing, 1950; Brian Roberts, 1977

TRIVIA:

The only other playoff series since 2000 that ended with a walk-off home run occurred in 2003. Aaron Boone's Game Seven, eleventh-inning homer gave the Yankees a 6-5 victory over the Red Sox and a World Series berth.

QUIZ:

What St. Louis Cardinal was the only pitcher to get a win in both the 1985 and 1987 World Series?

ANSWER: *John Tudor*

TODAY'S THOUGHT:

"Bob Gibson pitches as though he's double parked."
—Vin Scully

HISTORY:

On this date in 1968 Mickey Lolich won for the third time in the World Series as the Detroit Tigers defeated the St. Louis Cardinals, 4–1, in Game Seven. Lolich allowed just five runs in his three complete games, as the Tigers rallied after losing three of the first four contests.

BIRTHDAYS:

Gene Tenace, 1946; Placido Polanco, 1975; Pat Burrell, 1976; Noah Lowry, 1980

TRIVIA:

Bob Gibson matched Lolich with three complete games in the Series. Gibson won games one and four, but lost Game Seven. His consolation was a single-Series record of 35 strikeouts.

QUIZ:

This Cleveland Indians slugger set a major league record in 2006, hitting five grand-slams before the All-Star break. Name him.

ANSWER: *Travis Hafner*

TODAY'S THOUGHT:

"Baseball is a kids game that grownups only tried to screw up."
—*Bob Lemon*

HISTORY:

On this date in 1948 the Cleveland Indians, led by pitcher Bob Lemon, beat the Boston Braves 4-3 in Game Six of the World Series to win their final title of the century.

BIRTHDAYS:

Orlando Hernandez, 1965; Dmitri Young, 1973

TRIVIA:

Baseball is the only major American sport in which the championship trophy is not named after someone. Technically, it is known as the Commissioner's Trophy.

EXTRA INNING:

"Sure. I'm proud to be an American." –Cincinnati Reds pitcher *Steve Foster,* asked by a Canadian customs agent if he had anything to declare

QUIZ:

This Yankees manager won the pennant in his first three years at the helm. Who was he?

ANSWER: *Ralph Houk, in 1961, '62, and '63.*

TODAY'S THOUGHT:

"Almost the only place in life where a sacrifice is really appreciated." —*Mark Belaire*, on baseball

HISTORY:

On this date in 1986 Dave Henderson's two-run homer with Boston one strike away from elimination gave the Red Sox a 6-5 lead in Game Five of the AL Championship Series. After the Angels tied the game, Henderson's sacrifice fly in the eleventh inning gave the Sox a 7-6 win. Boston would win the pennant in seven games.

BIRTHDAYS:

Rick Ferrell, 1905; Joe Cronin, 1906; Sid Fernandez, 1962; Luis Polonia, 1963; Jose Valentin, 1969; Tanyon Sturtze, 1970

TRIVIA:

Donnie Moore, the Angels' pitcher who gave up the home run to Henderson, committed suicide three years later.

QUIZ:

On October 12, 1929, the largest comeback in a World Series game was made by what team?

ANSWER: *The Philadelphia Athletics, trailing 8-0 in Game Four, exploded for ten runs in the bottom of the seventh and defeated the Cubs, 10-8. The A's won the Series in five games.*

TODAY'S THOUGHT:

"It's not whether you win or lose, it's how you play the game."
—*Grantland Rice*

HISTORY:

On this date in 1960 Bill Mazeroski's lead-off home run in the bottom of the ninth inning of Game Seven of the World Series gave the Pirates a 10-9 win over the Yankees. For Pittsburgh, it was their first world championship in 35 years.

BIRTHDAYS:

Rube Waddell, 1876; Eddie Mathews, 1931; Trevor Hoffman, 1967

TRIVIA:

Ralph Terry, the losing pitcher in that game, later played golf on the Senior PGA Tour.

QUIZ:

In 1962, Yankees pitcher Ralph Terry was the first hurler to throw a complete game, 1-0 win in the seventh game of the World Series. He did it against the San Francisco Giants. Who was the losing pitcher?

ANSWER: *Jack Sanford*

TODAY'S THOUGHT:

"A complete ballplayer today is one who can hit, field, run, throw and pick the right agent." —*Robert Lurie*, owner of the San Francisco Giants

HISTORY:

On this date in 1905 Christy Mathewson pitched his third complete-game shutout of the World Series as the New York Giants beat the Philadelphia A's, 2-0, in Game Five to win the championship.

BIRTHDAYS:

Harry Brecheen, 1914; Tommy Harper, 1940; Al Oliver, 1946; Joe Girardi, 1964; Pat Kelly, 1967; Ryan Church, 1978; Duaner Sanchez, 1979

TRIVIA:

All five games of the 1905 World Series were shutouts. Along with Mathewson's three, Chief Bender of Philadelphia held the Giants scoreless in Game Two and the Giants' Joe McGinnity didn't allow a run in Game Four.

EXTRA INNING:

"I've been traveling so much I haven't had time to grow it." –Atlanta Braves third baseman *Bob Horner*, on why he no longer sported a beard

QUIZ:

Who is the only manager to win a World Series in both the American and National Leagues?

ANSWER: *Sparky Anderson, who led the Reds to titles in 1975 and '76 and the Tigers in 1984*

TODAY'S THOUGHT:

"If you don't get on first, you can't score a run." —*Enos Slaughter*

HISTORY:

On this date in 1946 in Game Seven of the World Series, St. Louis' Enos Slaughter raced home from first base on Harry Walker's hit to left-center field to give the Cardinals a 4-3 win over the Boston Red Sox.

BIRTHDAY:

Jim Palmer, 1945

TRIVIA:

The Houston Astros are the only team to have had Nolan Ryan, Roger Clemens, and Randy Johnson - the top three on the all-time strikeout list - on their roster at one time or another.

EXTRA INNING:

"I was trying to hit my in-laws." –Atlanta Braves pitcher *Greg Maddux*, on throwing a ball into the stands to celebrate his career-high fourteen strikeouts in a 1-0 win over Milwaukee.

QUIZ:

Ty Cobb, at .367, has the highest career batting average in major league history. Who's second?

ANSWER: *Rogers Hornsby, who hit .358*

TODAY'S THOUGHT:

"If Casey Stengel were alive today, he'd be spinning in his grave."
—*Ralph Kiner*

HISTORY:

On this date in 1969 the New York Mets, in just their eighth year of existence, became World Champions for the first time in franchise history. The Mets beat Baltimore, 5-3, in Game Five to complete a four games to one upset of the favored Orioles.

BIRTHDAYS:

Goose Goslin, 1900; Tim McCarver, 1941; Anthony Reyes, 1981

TRIVIA:

This date also marked two other World Series-clinching games. In 1962, the Yankees' Ralph Terry shut out the Giants, 1-0, in Game Seven to lead New York to their 20th title. In 1983, the Orioles' Scott McGregor pitched a five-hit shutout to beat the Phillies, 5-0, in Game Five for the championship.

QUIZ:

What player made the last out in the 1969 World Series?

ANSWER: *Davey Johnson, who, as manager, won a World Series ring with the Mets in 1986.*

TODAY'S THOUGHT:

"No matter who wins, this World Series will be remembered more for tragedy than triumph. The real heroes are the survivors and those who helped, not the ballplayers."
—*Brett Butler,* Giants outfielder

HISTORY:

On this date in 1989 an earthquake struck the Bay Area prior to game three of the World Series between the Oakland A's and San Francisco Giants, resulting in a ten-day delay in the Series. The A's would finish it off quickly after that, however, sweeping the Giants in four games.

BIRTHDAYS:

Buck Ewing, 1859; John Mabry, 1970; John Rocker, 1974

TRIVIA:

Out of respect for the tragic circumstances surrounding the 1989 World Series, the Athletics voted not to have any champagne in their clubhouse for their post-game celebration.

QUIZ:

What year was the first World Series game played in California? What teams were involved?

ANSWER: *The Los Angeles Dodgers and the Chicago White Sox went west with the World Series in 1959. LA took the title in six games.*

October 18

TODAY'S THOUGHT:

"I must admit, when Reggie Jackson hit his third home run and I was sure nobody was looking, I applauded in my glove."
—*Steve Garvey*, LA Dodgers infielder

HISTORY:

On this date in 1977 Reggie Jackson hit three home runs in three consecutive at-bats during Game Six of the World Series, giving the Yankees a series-clinching 8-4 victory over the Dodgers.

BIRTHDAYS:

Candy Cummings, 1848; Willie Horton, 1942; George Hendrick, 1949; Doug Mirabelli, 1970; Alex Cora, 1975

TRIVIA:

Each of Jackson's three homers came on the first pitches thrown by Burt Hooton, Elías Sosa and Charlie Hough. Mr. October drove in five runs in the game and earned Series MVP honors.

EXTRA INNING:

"If it turns out that Barry Bonds used steroids to bulk up and add muscle mass, he could get four to eight years as governor of California."
–Comedian *Argus Hamilton*

QUIZ:

Who is the only other player to hit three home runs in a single World Series game?

ANSWER: *Babe Ruth did it twice in the 1920s.*

TODAY'S THOUGHT:

"No presidential campaign can seriously begin until after the World Series." —*John F. Kennedy*

HISTORY:

On this date in 1981 Rick Monday hit a dramatic ninth-inning home run that gave LA a 2-1 win over the Montreal Expos in the deciding fifth game of the NLCS. The Dodgers would go on to beat the Yankees, four games to two, in the World Series.

BIRTHDAYS:

Mordecai "Three Finger" Brown, 1876; Sandy Alomar, 1943; Mark Davis, 1960; Tim Belcher, 1961; Keith Foulke, 1972; Michael Young, 1976

TRIVIA:

The 1981 World Series MVP Award was the first to be awarded to more than one player. It was split between Dodgers third baseman Ron Cey, outfielder Pedro Guerrero and catcher Steve Yeager.

EXTRA INNING:

"Tell Len I'm very proud of him. I hope he does better next time."
–*Tokie Lockhart*, after her grandson Len Barker pitched a perfect game

QUIZ:

What was the last team to lose back-to-back World Series?

ANSWER: *The Atlanta Braves, in 1991 to the Twins and '92 to the Blue Jays*

TODAY'S THOUGHT:

"We Americans are a peculiar people. We are for the underdog no matter how much of a dog he is."

—*Happy Chandler*, former baseball commissioner

HISTORY:

On this date in 2004 the Boston Red Sox became the first team in major league history to win a best-of-seven series after losing the first three games. Boston beat New York, 10-3, to win the AL Championship Series on the way to their first World Series title since 1918.

BIRTHDAYS:

Bruce Campbell, 1909; Mickey Mantle, 1931; Juan Marichal, 1937; Keith Hernandez, 1953; Juan Gonzalez, 1969

TRIVIA:

Another upset occurred on this day in 1988 when the Los Angeles Dodgers became World Champions by taking game five, 5-2, over the Oakland A's. Series MVP, Orel Hershiser, won two games in the Series.

QUIZ:

Who is the only man to have won the World Series MVP Award with two different teams?

ANSWER: *"Mr. October", Reggie Jackson, won it with the A's in 1973 and the Yankees in 1977.*

TODAY'S THOUGHT:

"Philadelphia is the only city where you can experience the thrill of victory and the agony of reading about it the next day."
—*Mike Schmidt*

HISTORY:

On this date in 1980 the third time was the charm for the Philadelphia Phillies. After losing the World Series in 1915 and 1950, the Phils won their first title, beating the Kansas City Royals in Game Six, 4-1.

BIRTHDAYS:

Whitey Ford, 1928; George Bell, 1959; Toby Hall, 1975; Khalil Greene, 1979

TRIVIA:

The '80 Fall Classic was the first World Series played entirely on artificial turf.

EXTRA INNING:

"There's been pressure on me since I was born. My parents wanted a girl."
–Relief pitcher *Lee Smith*

QUIZ:

What year saw the most total runs scored in a World Series?

ANSWER: *1960, when New York and Pittsburgh combined for 82 runs*

TODAY'S THOUGHT:

"All of the Mets' road wins against Los Angeles this year have been at Dodger Stadium." —*Ralph Kiner*

HISTORY:

On this date in 1972 and 1975 the Cincinnati Reds lost and won, respectively, Game Seven of the World Series. In '72, they fell to the A's, 3-2, as Oakland won their first of three consecutive championships. In '75, the Reds beat the Red Sox, 4-3, on a ninth-inning Joe Morgan single.

BIRTHDAYS:

Bill Carrigan, 1883; Jimmie Foxx, 1907; Wilbur Wood, 1941; Ichiro Suzuki, 1973; Michael Barrett, 1976; Robinson Cano, 1982

TRIVIA:

Oakland A's reliever Darold Knowles is the only man to have pitched in each game of a seven-game World Series. Knowles' name appeared in every box score in Oakland's Series triumph over the New York Mets in 1973.

QUIZ:

Who was the youngest player to throw a World Series shutout?

ANSWER: *Jim Palmer of the Orioles, at age 20, shut out the Dodgers, 6-0, in 1966.*

TODAY'S THOUGHT:

"Anyone who isn't either excited or nervous in a World Series is either crazy or a liar." —*Rogers Hornsby*

HISTORY:

On this date in 1993 the Blue Jays' Joe Carter hit the second walk-off homer in World Series history. His three-run shot off Phillies pitcher Mitch Williams gave Toronto an 8-6, Game Six victory for their second consecutive World Series title.

BIRTHDAYS:

Jim Bunning, 1931; Al Leiter, 1965; Kaz Matsui, 1975; John Lackey, 1978

TRIVIA:

Rather than retiring a number honoring players, the Blue Jays have instituted a "Level of Excellence" in the right and left-field areas at the Rogers Centre, where the likes of Joe Carter, Tony Fernandez and Dave Stieb are recognized.

QUIZ:

Mickey Mantle, Babe Ruth, and Yogi Berra are the top three home run hitters in World Series history. What non-Yankee is fourth?

ANSWER: *Duke Snider of the Dodgers, with 11*

TODAY'S THOUGHT:

"I played on clubs in San Diego and Atlanta where everybody liked each other. Everyone went to dinner together. And we finished in last place together." —*Cito Gaston*, on team chemistry

HISTORY:

On this date in 1992 the Toronto Blue Jays became the first World Series championship team from outside the United States. They defeated the Atlanta Braves, 4–3, in eleven innings in Game Six.

BIRTHDAYS:

Ron Gardenhire, 1957; Arthur Rhodes, 1969; Rafael Furcal, 1977

TRIVIA:

With the victory, Blue Jays' manager Cito Gaston became the first African-American manager to win a World Series.

EXTRA INNING:

"I wanted to go into my home-run trot, but I realized I didn't have one."
–*Jim Essian*, hitting his first home run in more than 100 games

QUIZ:

In 1992, who became the oldest player to get an extra base hit in the World Series?

ANSWER: *Dave Winfield, whose two-run double put the Blue Jays up in Game Six*

TODAY'S THOUGHT:

"I heard that Bill Buckner tried to commit suicide over the winter. He stepped in front of a car, but it went through his legs."
—*Billy Gardner*, on Buckner's error

HISTORY:

On this date in 1986 the New York Mets bunched three hits, a Boston wild pitch, and a grounder through the legs of Bill Buckner for a miraculous, come-from-behind 6-5 win over the Red Sox. The Mets' rally came with nobody on and two outs in the bottom of the tenth inning. Twice, they were one strike away from losing the Series.

BIRTHDAYS:

Lee MacPhail, 1917; Bobby Thomson, 1923; Pedro Martinez, 1971

TRIVIA:

With Boston moments away from a World Series title, the Shea Stadium scoreboard flashed the message, "CONGRATULATIONS RED SOX, 1986 WORLD SERIES CHAMPIONS."

QUIZ:

The two pitchers who recorded the final outs of the Mets' World Championships in 1969 and 1986 were once traded for one another. Who are they?

ANSWER: *Jerry Koosman of the '69 team was dealt to the Twins in 1978 for Jesse Orosco of the '86 team.*

TODAY'S THOUGHT:

"Baseball has prostituted itself. Pretty soon we'll be starting games at midnight so people in outer space can watch on prime time television." —*Ray Kroc*

HISTORY:

On this date in 2005 the Chicago White Sox completed a sweep of the Houston Astros with a 1–0, Game Four victory. It was Chicago's first trip to the Fall Classic since 1959, and the team's first championship since 1917.

BIRTHDAYS:

Frank Selee, 1859; Steve Rogers, 1949; Mike Hargrove, 1949; Francisco Liriano, 1983

TRIVIA:

The White Sox became the first team in World Series history to win two games on the same calendar date. Game Three, which went fourteen innings, ended at 1:19 a.m. Central Time on Wednesday, October 26. Game Four ended at 11:01 p.m. that night.

EXTRA INNING:

"I bought this very rare item- a tax form signed by Darryl Strawberry. This is the hottest thing out there now." –Comedian *Billy Crystal*

QUIZ:

In 2005, who became the first Houston Astro to hit a World Series home run?

ANSWER: *Mike Lamb, in Houston's 5-3, game one loss*

TODAY'S THOUGHT:

"What does a mama bear on the pill have in common with the World Series? No cubs." —*Harry Caray*

HISTORY:

On this date in 1991 Minnesota's Jack Morris pitched a ten-inning, 1-0, shutout against the Atlanta Braves in Game Seven of the World Series, giving the Twins their second championship in five years. Both Atlanta and Minnesota had finished last in their respective leagues the year before.

BIRTHDAYS:

Ralph Kiner, 1922; Bip Roberts, 1963; Brad Radke, 1972

TRIVIA:

Minnesota's 4.2 million square foot Mall of America, the largest shopping center in the nation, was built on the ground that housed the Twins' old Metropolitan Stadium.

EXTRA INNING:

"He gives new meaning to that term Big Red Machine." –Phillies pitcher *Larry Andersen*, on the weight of Cincinnati replacement pitcher Pedro Borbon.

QUIZ:

Where is the College World Series played?

ANSWER: *Omaha, Nebraska*

TODAY'S THOUGHT:

"When we played, World Series checks meant something. Now all they do is screw up your taxes." —*Don Drysdale*

HISTORY:

On this date in 1995 the Braves won their first World Series since moving to Atlanta in 1966. Tom Glavine and Mark Wohlers combined to pitch a one-hitter in Game Six, shutting out Cleveland, 1-0.

BIRTHDAYS:

Bob Veale, 1935; Lenny Harris, 1964; Juan Guzman, 1966; Braden Looper, 1974; Jeremy Bonderman, 1982

TRIVIA:

The 1995 World Series was televised by two different networks in the US. Games 1, 4, and 5 were televised by ABC, while NBC televised Games 2, 3, and 6.

QUIZ:

In 1996, Andruw Jones became the second player to hit home runs in his first two World Series at-bats. Can you name the first?

ANSWER: *Gene Tenace of the Oakland A's, versus the Reds in the first game of the 1972 Series*

TODAY'S THOUGHT:

"There are only two places in the league - first place and no place." —*Tom Seaver*

HISTORY:

On this date in 1969 New York's Tom Seaver, with a record of 25-7, won the first of his three NL Cy Young Awards. Four years later, Seaver would become the first person without twenty victories to win the award, going 19-10 for the season.

BIRTHDAYS:

Jesse Barfield, 1959; Karim Garcia, 1975

TRIVIA:

The "stuff" that umpires rub down baseballs with before each game is called Baltimore Clay.

EXTRA INNING:

"Most of us have such bad voices, we respect the national anthem by not singing it." –*Sparky Anderson*

QUIZ:

What brothers were the first to pitch against each other in an All-Star Game?

ANSWER: *Gaylord and Jim Perry faced off against each other in the 1970 All-Star Game in Cincinnati.*

TODAY'S THOUGHT:

"If he can't run for office any better than he runs the Texas Rangers, he don't have any advantage." —*Ed Martin*, Texas Democratic chairman, on George Dubya's run for governor of Texas

HISTORY:

On this date in 2001 George W. Bush, wearing an "FDNY" jacket to honor the heroes of September 11th, became the first president since Dwight Eisenhower to throw out the first pitch in a World Series game.

BIRTHDAYS:

Ed Delahanty, 1867; Bill Terry, 1898; Joe Adcock, 1927; Jim Perry, 1935; Jim Ray Hart, 1941; Danny Tartabull, 1962; Marco Scutaro, 1975; Luis Matos, 1978; Laynce Nix, 1980; Mike Jacobs, 1980

TRIVIA:

In 1990, George H.W. Bush became the first US president to throw out a first pitch on foreign soil, when the Texas Rangers faced off against the Blue Jays in Toronto's home opener. The Jays won the game, 2-1.

QUIZ:

Who was the first sitting president to attend a World Series game?

ANSWER: *Woodrow Wilson, at the 1915 World Series between the Phillies and the Red Sox*

TODAY'S THOUGHT:

"Attention Fans, Welcome to NOVEMBER BASEBALL." — Yankee Stadium scoreboard, at exactly 12 midnight on November 1, 2001 during Game 4 of the World Series

HISTORY:

On this date in 2001 the Yankees shocked the Diamondbacks in Game Four of the World Series when Tino Martinez hit a two-out, two-run homer in the bottom of the ninth inning to tie the score. That was followed in the tenth inning by Derek Jeter's solo homer to win the game, 3-2. Both home runs came off Arizona reliever Byung-Hyun Kim.

BIRTHDAYS:

Cal Hubbard, 1900; Dave McNally, 1942; Mickey Rivers, 1948; Fred McGriff, 1963; Steve Trachsel, 1970; David Dellucci, 1973

TRIVIA:

Byung-Hyun Kim became the first Korean-born player to play in the World Series.

QUIZ:

Three pitchers have the distinction of throwing a no-hitter, winning a Cy Young Award, and being named World Series MVP. Name them.

ANSWER: *Sandy Koufax, Bob Gibson and Bret Saberhagen*

TODAY'S THOUGHT:

"I've never seen anything like this." —*FOX commentator Tim McCarver*, on Scott Brosius' home run

HISTORY:

On this date in 2001 the first ever Major League Baseball game was started in November, and just like the night before, the Yankees staged an incredible World Series comeback against Arizona. Scott Brosius' one-out, two-run homer in the ninth tied the game at two, and Alfonso Soriano won the game in the bottom of the twelfth with an RBI single. The losing pitcher? Byun-Hyung Kim...again.

BIRTHDAYS:

Bid McPhee, 1859; Fernando Valenzuela, 1960; Coco Crisp, 1979

TRIVIA:

Diamondbacks manager Bob Brenley had announced the World Series the previous year with John Buck and Tim McCarver on FOX.

QUIZ:

What World Series winner finished the regular season with a record of 85-77, the worst mark of any team to win a title?

ANSWER: *The 1987 Minnesota Twins, who beat the St. Louis Cardinals in seven games to win the Series*

TODAY'S THOUGHT:

"You know I signed with the Milwaukee Brewers for $3,000. That bothered my dad at the time, because he didn't have that kind of dough to pay out. But eventually he scraped it up." —*Bob Uecker*

HISTORY:

On this date in 1974 the Atlanta Braves traded Hank Aaron to the Milwaukee Brewers for outfielder Dave May and a minor-leaguer. Aaron would finish his major league career in Milwaukee, where he started with the Braves in 1954.

BIRTHDAYS:

Travis Jackson, 1903; Tom Paciorek, 1946; Willie McGee, 1958; Orlando Cabrera, 1974; Sidney Ponson, 1976

TRIVIA:

Aaron made his final appearance in a Braves uniform that same day, when he squared off against Japan's Sadaharu Oh in a home run derby in Tokyo. Aaron took the contest, 10-9.

EXTRA INNING:

"That's the great thing about baseball. You never know what's going on."
–*Ralph Kiner*

QUIZ:

What team were the Milwaukee Brewers known as in 1969?

ANSWER: *The Seattle Pilots - They became the Brewers after just one season.*

TODAY'S THOUGHT:

"Every great batter works on the theory that the pitcher is more afraid of him than he is of the pitcher." —*Ty Cobb*

HISTORY:

On this date in 1926 American League umpire and former Tigers infielder George Moriarty replaced Ty Cobb as Detroit's manager. Because Moriarty had also been a scout for the team, he became the first man in history to hold four principal jobs in Major League Baseball.

BIRTHDAYS:

Bob Feller, 1918; Ken Holtzman, 1945; Bob Welch, 1956; Armando Benitez, 1972

TRIVIA:

Pete Rose was the last player-manager in the majors. After being traded from the Expos to the Reds in August of 1984, Rose was immediately given the position, replacing Vern Rapp. In his final two years in baseball, Rose led Cincinnati to two second-place finishes in the division.

QUIZ:

Since the Manager of the Year Award was given out in 1983, only one skipper has won the honor in back-to-back years. Who?

ANSWER: *The Atlanta Braves' Bobby Cox, in 2004 and '05*

TODAY'S THOUGHT:

"Not only will I be changing diapers at home, now I will be changing them in the clubhouse." —*Jim Eisenreich*, on his wife giving birth while he was playing on a young Florida Marlins team

HISTORY:

On this date in 2001 in a classic Game Seven, the Arizona Diamondbacks, with an RBI single by Luis Gonzalez in the bottom of the ninth, rallied to beat the Yankees, 3-2, earning their first World Series Championship in franchise history.

BIRTHDAYS:

Bobby Wallace, 1873; Dick Groat, 1930; Eric Karros, 1967; Carlos Baerga, 1968; Larry Bigbie, 1977

TRIVIA:

The four-year-old Diamondbacks became the first professional sports team in Arizona to win a title. In doing so, they ended the Yankees' streak of three consecutive World Championships.

QUIZ:

In 1997, when Florida defeated Cleveland in Game Seven for their first title, what Marlin delivered the winning hit in the bottom of the eleventh?

ANSWER: *Shortstop Edgar Renteria - His single up the middle scored Craig Counsell and gave the Fish a 3-2 win.*

TODAY'S THOUGHT:

"I can tell my grandchildren that I pitched to John Kennedy at Harvard." —*Lew Krause*, after the Red Sox worked out at Harvard and he pitched to Sox utility player, John Kennedy

HISTORY:

On this date in 1940 Walter Johnson's attempt to go from Senator to the House of Representatives fell short. The Hall of Fame pitcher for Washington had been elected as the Montgomery County Commissioner in 1938, but went down in defeat as the Republican candidate for Congress from Maryland.

BIRTHDAYS:

Harry Gumbert, 1909; Javy Lopez, 1970; Johnny Damon, 1973

TRIVIA:

John Kennedy, as in Today's Thought, actually shares the same birthday as JFK, May 29. John Kennedy was also a Senator in Washington, a baseball Senator, that is.

QUIZ:

Name the Hall of Famer who was Rookie of the Year in 1959 despite playing in only 59 games.

ANSWER: *San Francisco Giants first baseman Willie McCovey hit .354 with 13 home runs and 38 RBIs to earn the award.*

TODAY'S THOUGHT:

"Rich Folkers is throwing up in the bullpen." —*Jerry Coleman*

HISTORY:

On this date in 1974 the Los Angeles Dodgers' Mike Marshall became the first relief pitcher to win the Cy Young Award. Marshall set major league records with 106 appearances and 208 innings pitched in relief, surpassing his own marks.

BIRTHDAYS:

Walter Johnson, 1887; John Candelaria, 1953; Chad Curtis, 1968; Devi Cruz, 1972; Adam LaRoche, 1979

TRIVIA:

The Dodgers' nickname originated in Brooklyn in the 1890s, when trolley cars were the basic mode of public transportation and natives were forced to "dodge" trolleys in the city's busy streets. The nickname later followed the team to California.

QUIZ:

What's the name of the park where the annual Baseball Hall of Fame game is played?

ANSWER: *Abner Doubleday Field*

TODAY'S THOUGHT:

"I just won the Nobel Prize of baseball." —*Elston Howard*, on being named 1963 American League MVP

HISTORY:

On this date in 1963 Elston Howard was named the Most Valuable Player in the American League. The Yankees catcher hit .287 with 28 homers and 85 RBIs as the first black MVP in league history.

BIRTHDAYS:

Jim Kaat, 1938; Joe Niekro, 1944; Kris Benson, 1974

TRIVIA:

Jim Kaat, who had a distinguished 25-year run in the majors, set a record for pitchers with sixteen Gold Gloves.

EXTRA INNING:

"They should have called a welder." –Richie Ashburn, on Dave Kingman's glove being repaired

QUIZ:

There have been two pitchers who have struck out as many batters in a big league game as their age. Can you name them?

ANSWER: *Bob Feller, 17, and Kerry Wood, 20*

TODAY'S THOUGHT:

"Just look at him over there. Doesn't drink, doesn't smoke, doesn't take greenies... hits the hell out of the ball, hustles like crazy, plays a great centerfield and isn't trying to get anything from anybody... Doesn't he just make you sick?" —*Terry Forster,* on Dale Murphy

HISTORY:

On this date in 1983 Atlanta Braves outfielder Dale Murphy was named the National League MVP for the second straight season. He joined Ernie Banks, Joe Morgan and Mike Schmidt as players who won the award in consecutive years.

BIRTHDAYS:

Bucky Harris, 1896; Henry Rodriguez, 1967; Jose Offerman, 1968; Edgardo Alfonzo, 1973

TRIVIA:

The Yankees have won more MVPs than any team in baseball history, including three three-time winners Yogi Berra, Mickey Mantle, and Joe DiMaggio.

QUIZ:

What player made history on November 8, 1966, when he became the first person to win MVPs in both the AL and the NL?

ANSWER: *Frank Robinson, in 1961 with Cincinnati and in 1966 with Baltimore*

TODAY'S THOUGHT:

"Wasn't watching." —*Phil Rizzuto*, broadcaster, when asked what "ww" stood for in his score book following an at-bat

HISTORY:

On this date in 1995 Dodgers pitching ace Hideo Nomo became the first Japanese player to win a major American baseball award when he was named the National League Rookie of the Year. Nomo went 13-6 with a 2.54 ERA for Los Angeles.

BIRTHDAYS:

Bob Gibson, 1935; Adam Dunn, 1979

TRIVIA:

When LA's Todd Hollandsworth won the NL Rookie of the Year in 1996, it marked the fifth consecutive time that the award went to a Dodger player. The previous winners were Eric Karros (1992), Mike Piazza ('93), Raúl Mondesí ('94), and of course, Nomo.

QUIZ:

The 1993 movie *Rookie of the Year* tells the fictional story of a twelve year-old sensation pitching for what major league team?

ANSWER: *The Chicago Cubs*

TODAY'S THOUGHT:

"He has enough power to hit home runs in any park - including Yellowstone." —*Paul Richards*, on Harmon Killebrew

HISTORY:

On this date in 1975 the Kansas City Royals released slugger Harmon Killebrew after his one year with the team, ending a twenty-two year Hall of Fame career highlighted by 573 home runs

BIRTHDAYS:

Norm Cash, 1934; Jack Clark, 1955; Kenny Rogers, 1964; Shawn Green, 1972

TRIVIA:

In 1962, when Killebrew led the league in runs batted in with 126, his .243 batting average was the lowest ever for an RBI champion. Nine years later, he again led the league in RBIs (119) and hit only .254 - the third-lowest average ever for an RBI king.

EXTRA INNING:

"I didn't do so great in the first grade either." –*Dizzy Dean*, on quitting school after the second grade

QUIZ:

In the 1990s, what two Kansas City Royals were named Rookie of the Year?

ANSWER: *Bob Hamelin, in 1994, and Carlos Beltran, in 1999*

TODAY'S THOUGHT:

"That space between the white lines, that's my office. That's where I conduct my business." —*Early Wynn*

HISTORY:

On this date in 2001 Cardinals slugger Mark McGwire announced his retirement. Big Mac declined a two-year, $30 million extension, explaining that he could not "perform at a level equal to the salary the organization would be paying me."

BIRTHDAYS:

Rabbit Maranville, 1891; Pie Traynor, 1899; Hal Trosky, 1912; Roberto Hernandez, 1964; Damion Easley, 1969; Rey Ordonez, 1971

TRIVIA:

McGwire's brother, Dan, played quarterback for the Seattle Seahawks in the early '90s. He was a first round pick in the 1991 NFL draft, selected ahead of Brett Favre. Dan, at 6'8", was the tallest quarterback in NFL history.

QUIZ:

In 1981, this future Pro Football Hall of Fame quarterback signed a minor league contract as an outfielder with the New York Yankees. Name him.

ANSWER: *John Elway*

TODAY'S THOUGHT:

"Sporting goods companies pay me not to endorse their products." —*Bob Uecker*

HISTORY:

On this date in 1920 Major League Baseball's owners elected United States District Court Judge Kenesaw Mountain Landis as the sport's first commissioner. The action came in response to the Black Sox scandal and the disapproval of former AL President Ban Johnson's ruling on it.

BIRTHDAYS:

Carl Mays, 1891; Bruce Bochte, 1950; Sammy Sosa, 1968; Aaron Heilman, 1978

TRIVIA:

Peter Ueberroth, who served as baseball's commissioner from 1984 to '89, was the chairman of the Los Angeles Olympic Organizing Committee for the 1984 Summer Games. Due to the success and profits gained from the Games, Ueberroth was named *Time* magazine's "Man of the Year."

QUIZ:

When was the last time two baseball players were named co-"Sportsmen of the Year" by *Sports Illustrated*?

ANSWER: *In 2001, when the Diamondbacks' Curt Schilling and Randy Johnson won the award*

TODAY'S THOUGHT:

"Nobody taught Joe DiMaggio how to hit. I refuse to take any credit for him. I was just smart enough to leave him alone."
—Lefty O'Doul

HISTORY:

On this date in 1951 Lefty O'Doul's all-stars, including major leaguers Joe DiMaggio and Billy Martin, were beaten, 3–1, by an all-star team in Tokyo. It was the first time that an American professional team had lost to a Japanese team.

BIRTHDAYS:

Steve Bilko, 1928; Mel Stottlemyre, 1941; Pat Hentgen, 1968

TRIVIA:

Lefty O'Doul won NL batting titles in 1929 and 1932, but was equally as successful after his playing career. As a manager in the minor leagues with the San Francisco Seals, he helped develop Joe DiMaggio. He then gained fame in Japan when he served as baseball's goodwill ambassador before and after World War II.

QUIZ:

Who was the last player to win back-to-back league batting titles?

ANSWER: *Nomar Garciaparra of the Red Sox, in 1999 and 2000*

TODAY'S THOUGHT:

"Sorry Mickey, but because of the way you lived on Earth, you can't come in. But, before you leave, would you autograph these baseballs for HIM?" —*Mickey Mantle,* quoting St. Peter at the Pearly Gates

HISTORY:

On this date in 1956 Mickey Mantle was the unanimous choice as the American League MVP. The announcement was not a surprise, since Mantle won the Triple Crown with a .353 average, 52 home runs, and 130 runs batted in.

BIRTHDAYS:

Curt Schilling, 1966; Xavier Nady, 1978

TRIVIA:

That year, Mantle became the first Yankee other than Babe Ruth to hit 50 home runs in a season. For his efforts, The Mick won the Hickok Belt, given to the top professional athlete of the year in any sport. The award, first presented in 1950, was discontinued in 1976.

QUIZ:

Who was the last person to win baseball's Triple Crown?

ANSWER: *Carl Yastrzemski, who in 1967 hit .326 with 44 home runs and 121 RBIs for the Boston Red Sox*

TODAY'S THOUGHT:

"More than anyone else, he's made me wish I wasn't a manager." —*Walter Alston*, on Hank Aaron

HISTORY:

On this date in 2004 the Giants' Barry Bonds became the oldest MVP Award winner at the age of forty. Bonds hit .362 with 45 homers and 101 RBIs to capture his fourth consecutive award and seventh overall. No one else has more than three.

BIRTHDAYS:

Pat Ragan, 1888; Gus Bell, 1928

TRIVIA:

Hank Aaron, who played briefly with the Indianapolis Clowns, was the last Negro Leaguer to play in the major leagues. He got his start in 1954 when a spring training injury to Bobby Thomson opened up a spot on the Braves roster.

QUIZ:

Who's the only American League player since 1990 to win back-to-back MVP Awards?

ANSWER: *Frank Thomas of the White Sox, who was the AL MVP in 1993 and '94*

TODAY'S THOUGHT:

"Maybe two Young Awards should be presented each year - the Cy for the best pitcher and the Anthony for the worst." —*Allan Malamud*, sportswriter, on Anthony Young, who lost 27 straight games

HISTORY:

On this date in 1998 the Blue Jays' Roger Clemens became the first pitcher to win five Cy Young Awards, his third with Toronto. Clemens led all AL pitchers in wins (20), strikeouts (271) and ERA (2.65). Two trophies came later with the Yankees (2001) and Astros (2004).

BIRTHDAYS:

Dwight Gooden, 1964; Julio Lugo, 1975

TRIVIA:

Roger Clemens and his wife, Debbie, have four sons: Koby, Kory, Kacy, and Kody (Ks as in strikeouts). Koby was drafted by the Astros as a third baseman in 2005 at the age of eighteen.

QUIZ:

What promising Houston Astros pitcher suffered a career-ending stroke in 1980?

ANSWER: *JR Richard, who won at least 18 games in each of the four seasons before his career was cut short*

TODAY'S THOUGHT:

"Talent always beats experience. Because by the time you get experience, the talent's gone." —*Pat Corrales*, Indians manager

HISTORY:

On this date in 1992 the National League's two newest teams, the Colorado Rockies and Florida Marlins, held their expansion drafts. Noteworthy selections included Trevor Hoffman and Jeff Conine for Florida, and Joe Girardi and Vinny Castilla for Colorado.

BIRTHDAYS:

Mike Garcia, 1923; Jim Brewer, 1937; Tom Seaver, 1944; Mitch Williams, 1964; Jeff Nelson, 1966

TRIVIA:

Gary Sheffield, who was traded from San Diego to the Marlins for Trevor Hoffman, had gold inlays on his front teeth until his rookie season with the Brewers, when he had them removed to portray a better image.

QUIZ:

Before the A's moved to Oakland, their Kansas City home featured Charlie Finley's "Pennant Porch." Can you name that ballpark?

ANSWER: *Municipal Stadium*

TODAY'S THOUGHT:

"Trying to hit him was like trying to drink coffee with a fork."
—*Willie Stargell*, on Sandy Koufax

HISTORY:

On this date in 1966 Dodgers ace Sandy Koufax announced his retirement from Major League Baseball at the age of thirty. Increasing pain in his arthritic left elbow forced the southpaw to call it a career, despite winning 27 games that season and three consecutive Cy Young Awards.

BIRTHDAYS:

Jack Coombs, 1882; Roy Sievers, 1926; Jamie Moyer, 1962; Dante Bichette, 1963; Tom Gordon, 1967; David Ortiz, 1975

TRIVIA:

Koufax ended his career as one of the few pitchers with more career strike-outs than innings pitched, a feat equaled only by Nolan Ryan, Pedro Martinez, and Randy Johnson. In 2,324 innings, Koufax struck out 2,396 batters, an average of 9.69 Ks per nine innings.

QUIZ:

In the 1990s, what starting pitcher set a single-season major league record by averaging 12.58 strikeouts per nine innings for the year?

ANSWER: *Kerry Wood, in 1998*

TODAY'S THOUGHT:

"I've been treated there just like everywhere else: you got everyone booing for you. I take that as a compliment." —*Albert Belle*, on Orioles Park at Camden Yards in Baltimore

HISTORY:

On this date in 1996 two of baseball's most controversial figures, White Sox owner Jerry Reinsdorf and former Indians slugger Albert Belle, came to terms on a 5-year contract worth $55 million. Belle's deal with Chicago made him the first player in MLB history to earn $10 million a season.

BIRTHDAYS:

Roy Campanella, 1921; Ted Turner, 1938; Bob Boone, 1947; Justin Duchscherer, 1977; Ryan Howard, 1979

TRIVIA:

In 1995, Belle became the first player to hit fifty home runs and fifty doubles in the same season.

QUIZ:

Only two American Leaguers have won the home run title six or more times. One was Babe Ruth. Do you know the other?

ANSWER: *Harmon Killebrew wore the crown six times between 1959 and 1969.*

TODAY'S THOUGHT:

"I wish he were still playing. I'd probably crack his head open to show him how valuable I was." —*Roger Clemens*, after hearing Hank Aaron say that pitchers should not be eligible for the MVP Award

HISTORY:

On this date in 1990 Boston's Roger Clemens was suspended for the first five games of the 1991 season and fined $10,000 due to his unsportsmanlike behavior toward the umpires in Game Four of the AL Championship Series. His club was swept by the A's.

BIRTHDAYS:

Clark Griffith, 1869; Rick Monday, 1945; Gabe White, 1971; J.D. Drew, 1975

TRIVIA:

In 1951, umpire Frank Dascoli ejected the entire Dodgers' bench after a protest over a controversial call at home. Among those thrown out was Bill Sharman, who became the first major leaguer ejected without ever playing in a single game. Yes, the same Bill Sharman that had a Hall of Fame career with the NBAs Boston Celtics.

QUIZ:

What pitcher threw a no-hitter against the Padres in 1970 and later claimed to have been high on LSD and amphetamines throughout the game?

ANSWER: *Dock Ellis, as a member of the Pirates*

TODAY'S THOUGHT:

"Every time I sign a ball, and there have been thousands, I thank my luck that I wasn't born Coveleski or Wambsganss or Peckinpaugh." —*Mel Ott*

HISTORY:

On this date in 1958 and 1988 Major League Baseball lost two of its all-time greats. In an eerie coincidence, Hall of Famers Mel Ott and Carl Hubbell, who spent their entire careers with the New York Giants and were teammates for 16 years, died exactly 30 years apart due to injuries resulting from car accidents. Ott died in 1958 at age forty-nine, and Hubbell in 1988 at eighty-five.

BIRTHDAYS:

Bobby Mathews, 1851; Freddie Lindstrom, 1905; Stan Musial, 1920; Ken Griffey, Jr., 1969; Hank Blalock, 1980

TRIVIA:

In 1944, Carl Hubbell was the first National Leaguer to have his number retired. Both Hubbell's number 11 and Ott's number 4 are on the facing of the upper deck near left field at San Francisco's A&T Park along with the numbers of other Giants greats.

QUIZ:

The Pittsburgh Pirates retired Honus Wagner's number 33- a number that he wore as a coach, but never as a player. Why?

ANSWER: *They didn't wear uniform numbers in Wagner's playing days.*

TODAY'S THOUGHT:

"He was the best one-legged player I ever saw play the game."
—*Casey Stengel*, on Mickey Mantle

HISTORY:

On this date in 1957 in a controversial vote, Mickey Mantle edged out Ted Williams, 233 votes to 209, to win the AL MVP Award. Williams led the league in batting average and home runs, but Mantle's Yankees finished in first place while the Red Sox came in third.

BIRTHDAYS:

Dick Bartell, 1907; Lew Burdette, 1926; Greg Luzinski, 1950; Jay Payton, 1972; Ricky Ledee, 1973; Joe Nathan, 1974; Jonny Gomes, 1980

TRIVIA:

Ted Williams won the Triple Crown in 1942 and 1947. However, he failed to win the American League Most Valuable Player Award in either of those years, losing out to the Yankees' Joe Gordon and Joe DiMaggio, respectively. Williams did win the AL MVP in 1946 and '49.

QUIZ:

Who's the first player from a last-place team to win the MVP?

ANSWER: *Chicago Cubs outfielder Andre Dawson, who in 1987 was named the NL MVP after hitting .287 and leading the league in home runs (49) and RBI (137)*

TODAY'S THOUGHT:

"I'm going to write a book - *How to Make a Small Fortune in Baseball.* You start with a large fortune." —*Ruly Carpenter*, former Phillies owner

HISTORY:

On this date in 1943 Phillies owner William D. Cox was banned from baseball for life by Commissioner Kenesaw Mountain Landis after it was discovered Cox bet on his team to win games.

BIRTHDAYS:

Jack McKeon, 1930; Luis Tiant, 1940; Adam Eaton, 1977; Jonathan Papelbon, 1980

TRIVIA:

The team name, "Phillies", is the longest continuous use of a nickname in American pro sports. However, it was almost changed in the 1940s after ownership switched hands. The name "Blue Jays" was chosen from a contest, and stood as the unofficial team name for one year until it was abandoned in 1946.

QUIZ:

In 1990, Commissioner Fay Vincent refused to allow the White Sox to place what sixty-seven year-old on their roster?

ANSWER: *Minnie Minoso, who was hoping to appear in a professional game in a sixth consecutive decade*

TODAY'S THOUGHT:

"Enos Cabell started out with the Astros, and before that he was with the Orioles." —*Jerry Coleman*

HISTORY:

On this date in 1972 the New York Yankees acquired Matty Alou from the Oakland Athletics for Rob Gardner. Ironically, the previous year the Yankees traded Gardner to the A's for another Alou, Matty's brother Felipe.

BIRTHDAYS:

George Burns, 1889; Joe Medwick, 1911; Randy Velarde, 1962; Al Martin, 1967; Horacio Ramirez, 1979; Jose Lopez, 1983

TRIVIA:

Felipe Alou was the first Dominican to play regularly in the major leagues. Three of the four Alous that played pro ball (Felipe, younger brother Matty, and Felipe's son Moises) were named All-Stars multiple times. Only Jesus, Felipe's other brother, failed to earn the honor.

QUIZ:

The 1970 AL batting champion had a brother who gained 1,000 yards in the NFL that same year. Can you name these talented siblings?

ANSWER: *Alex Johnson, who hit .329 for the Angels and brother, Ron, of the New York Giants*

TODAY'S THOUGHT:

"If anything prepares you to be president, it's being a Red Sox fan."
—*John Kerry*

HISTORY:

On this date in 2002 the Boston Red Sox signed twenty-eight year-old Theo Epstein as their new general manager. Epstein, a life-long Red Sox fan who grew up just a mile from Fenway Park, became the youngest GM in baseball history.

BIRTHDAYS:

Joe DiMaggio, 1914; Bucky Dent, 1951; Octavio Dotel, 1973; Nick Swisher, 1980

TRIVIA:

Epstein's grandfather, Philip, and great-uncle, Julius, wrote the Oscar-winning screenplay for *Casablanca*.

QUIZ:

The ending to what 2005 movie about the Boston Red Sox had to be rewritten after the real-life Sox won the 2004 World Series?

ANSWER: Fever Pitch, *starring Jimmy Fallon and Drew Barrymore*

TODAY'S THOUGHT:

"Rookie Wilson was candidate for Mookie of the Year."
—*Ralph Kiner*, on Mookie Wilson

HISTORY:

On this date in 1975 Boston Red Sox center fielder Fred Lynn became the first major leaguer to earn Rookie of the Year and MVP honors in the same season. Lynn batted .331 with 21 home runs and 105 RBIs.

BIRTHDAYS:

Hugh Duffy, 1866; Bob Johnson, 1905; Lefty Gomez, 1908; Bob Elliot, 1916; Richie Hebner, 1947; Harold Reynolds, 1960; Chuck Finley, 1962; Brian Schneider, 1976

TRIVIA:

In 2001, Seattle Mariners' outfielder Ichiro Suzuki became the second player to win both awards. He was also the first rookie to lead all players in voting for the All-Star Game, thanks in large part to Major League Baseball's allowance of voting in Japan.

QUIZ:

Who was the first Japanese player to appear in a major league game?

ANSWER: *Masanori Murakami, a reliever who made his debut in 1964 for the Giants*

TODAY'S THOUGHT:

"Once he hit a line drive right past my ear. I turned around and saw the ball hit his ass sliding into second." —*Satchel Paige*, on the speed of Cool Papa Bell

HISTORY:

On this date in 1997 Negro League legend Buck Leonard died at the age of ninety. Leonard teamed with fellow power hitter and Hall of Famer Josh Gibson to lead the Homestead Grays to nine consecutive Negro National League titles from 1937 to '45.

BIRTHDAYS:

Dave Giusti, 1939; Mike Scioscia, 1958; Ivan Rodriguez, 1971; Jimmy Rollins, 1978

TRIVIA:

Both Gibson and Leonard rank in the Top 50 of "The 100 Greatest Baseball Players," a poll conducted by *The Sporting News*. The duo was dubbed the "Thunder Twins" by black newspapers and Leonard, a first baseman who batted fourth in the lineup behind Gibson, was referred to as the "Black Lou Gehrig."

QUIZ:

What Negro League team did Jackie Robinson play with briefly before joining the Dodgers?

ANSWER: *Kansas City Monarchs*

TODAY'S THOUGHT:

"I enjoy being a reliever because I like getting six outs for the same money as getting twenty seven." —*Steve McCatty*

HISTORY:

On this date in 2005 Toronto Blue Jays general manager J.P Ricciardi signed former Baltimore Orioles pitcher B.J. Ryan to the richest contract ever for a reliever, a 5-year, $47 million deal.

BIRTHDAYS:

Dave Righetti, 1958; Walt Weiss, 1963; Matt Williams, 1965; Robb Nen, 1969; Pedro Astacio, 1969

TRIVIA:

Bill Singer is the pitcher credited with baseball's first save. The statistic made its debut in 1969 when Singer was playing with the Dodgers, and history was made in a 3-2 Los Angeles win over the Reds.

QUIZ:

Who is the only closer in baseball history to win the MVP Award, Cy Young Award, and a World Series ring in the same year?

ANSWER: *Willie Hernandez, who in 1984 converted 32 of 33 saves with a 1.92 ERA and won a title with the Detroit Tigers*

TODAY'S THOUGHT:

"I'll probably get a million more than I should, but I didn't make the rules. I'm just taking advantage of them."
—*Reggie Jackson*, on becoming a free agent

HISTORY:

On this date in 1976 following his one year with the Orioles, the Yankees signed free-agent outfielder Reggie Jackson to a five-year, $3.5 million contract. During Mr. October's five-year stint with the club, the Bronx Bombers would win four divisions, three pennants, and two World Series.

BIRTHDAYS:

Minnie Minoso, 1922; Howard Johnson, 1960; Mariano Rivera, 1969

TRIVIA:

Jackson was the first player in MLB history to hit 100 home runs with three different teams: the A's, Angels and Yankees.

EXTRA INNING:

"He'd give you the shirt off his back. Of course, he'd call a press conference to announce it." –*Catfish Hunter*, on Reggie Jackson

QUIZ:

In 2000, what relief pitcher, who wore the number 99, signed a three-year, $9,999,999.99 contract with the New York Mets?

ANSWER: *Turk Wendell*

TODAY'S THOUGHT:

"Luck is the residue of design." —*Branch Rickey*

HISTORY:

On this date in 1887 the first indoor softball game was played in Chicago, Illinois. George Hancock, a reporter for the Chicago Board of Trade, invented the game and intended it to be a winter version of baseball. He used a stuffed boxing glove for the ball and a broomstick handle as a bat.

BIRTHDAYS:

Bo Jackson, 1962; Ray Durham, 1971; Craig Wilson, 1976; Rich Harden, 1981

TRIVIA:

The score of a forfeited softball game is 7-0.

QUIZ:

What team did the United States women's softball team defeat to win the gold medal at the 2004 Summer Olympics in Athens?

ANSWER: *Australia*

TODAY'S THOUGHT:

"Look at misfortune the same way you look at success: Don't panic. Do your best and forget the consequences."
—*Walter Alston*

HISTORY:

On this date in 1931 a pair of future Hall of Famers were traded for one another when the Chicago Cubs dealt Hack Wilson, along with pitcher Bud Teachout, to the St. Louis Cardinals for Burleigh Grimes. The Cardinals then traded Wilson to the Dodgers before the start of the 1932 season.

BIRTHDAYS:

Ed Reulbach, 1882; Walter Alston, 1911; George Foster, 1948; Larry Walker, 1966; Reggie Sanders, 1967; Kirk Rueter, 1970

TRIVIA:

Hack Wilson received his nickname because of his resemblance to an internationally famous Russian weightlifter named George Hackenschmidt. Despite being just 5′6″, Wilson weighed 195 pounds and had an 18″ neck. His shoe size, though, was only a six.

QUIZ:

Who was the last major leaguer to get at least 160 RBIs in a single season?

ANSWER: *The Cubs' Sammy Sosa, with 160 in 2001*

TODAY'S THOUGHT:

"This is truly an international event. We signed an outstanding Mexican pitcher at an Italian restaurant in the middle of Chinatown." *—Dodgers VP Al Campanis*, on the signing of Fernando Valenzuela

HISTORY:

On this date in 1981 after a strike-shortened season, LA Dodgers pitcher Fernando Valenzuela was named the National League Rookie of the Year. Valenzuela had been named earlier as the NL Cy Young Award winner, becoming the first player in major league history to win both awards in the same season.

BIRTHDAYS:

Darryl Kile, 1968; Mark Kotsay, 1975

TRIVIA:

Valenzuela became the third consecutive Dodger to earn NL Rookie of the Year honors. The previous winners were Rick Sutcliffe (1979) and Steve Howe (1980). Second baseman Steve Sax continued the trend in 1982, making it four years in a row for LA.

QUIZ:

Who is the only pitcher in major league history to win back-to-back Most Valuable Player Awards?

ANSWER: *The Tigers' Hal Newhouser won it in 1944 and '45.*

TODAY'S THOUGHT:

"Being traded is like celebrating your hundredth birthday. It might not be the happiest occasion in the world, but consider the alternatives." —*Joe Garagiola*

HISTORY:

On this date in 1933 Philadelphia A's owner Connie Mack sold catcher Mickey Cochrane to Detroit for $100,000. Economic reasons forced Mack to sell off his many stars, including Lefty Grove. As a result, the team that won 107 games in 1931 was in last place by 1935.

BIRTHDAYS:

Darryl Hamilton, 1964; Paul Byrd, 1970

TRIVIA:

In 1962, the New York Mets acquired Harry Chiti for a player to be named later. That player to be named later was- Harry Chiti.

EXTRA INNING:

"Ability is the act of getting credit for all the home runs someone else hits." –*Casey Stengel*

QUIZ:

The Cardinals traded pitcher Steve Carlton to Philadelphia in 1972, where he went on to win four Cy Young Awards. What pitcher did St. Louis get in return?

ANSWER: *Rick Wise*

TODAY'S THOUGHT:

"Never let your head hang down. Never give up and sit down and grieve. Find another way. And don't pray when it rains if you don't pray when the sun shines." —*Satchel Paige*

HISTORY:

On this date in 1943 at Major League Baseball's annual winter meetings, Commissioner Kenesaw Mountain Landis declared, "Each club is entirely free to employ Negro players to any extent it pleases." It would be over three years before the Dodgers introduced Jackie Robinson to the big leagues.

BIRTHDAYS:

Jesse Burkett, 1868; Bob Shawkey, 1890; Harvey Kuenn, 1930; Lee Smith, 1957; Tadahito Iguchi, 1974; Kyle Lohse, 1978; Gustavo Chacin, 1980; Jerome Williams, 1981

TRIVIA:

Landis was elected to the Baseball Hall of Fame in 1944 in a special election held one month after his death. The official title of each league's Most Valuable Player Award is the "Kenesaw Mountain Landis Award."

QUIZ:

What's the greatest amount of pitches a batter can face, without ever lifting the bat off his shoulder, until he either strikes out or walks?

ANSWER: *Eleven - He's at the plate with a 3-2 count when a base runner gets caught stealing for the third out. He then comes up the next inning and either walks or strikes out following another 3-2 count.*

TODAY'S THOUGHT:

"Doctors tell me I have the body of a thirty year-old. I know I have the brain of a fifteen year-old. If you've got both, you can play baseball." —*Pete Rose*

HISTORY:

On this date in 1978 Pete Rose signed a four-year, $3.2 million contract with the Philadelphia Phillies. Rose had spent the first sixteen years of his career with the Cincinnati Reds.

BIRTHDAY:

Cliff Floyd, 1972

TRIVIA:

Pete Rose pulled military duty at the end of the 1963 baseball season, when he was assigned to Fort Knox. Later on, Charlie Hustle served as a company cook while with a reserve unit at Fort Thomas.

EXTRA INNING:

"There is no homework." –*Dan Quisenberry*, on the best thing about baseball

QUIZ:

In what countries has Major League Baseball played regular season games?

ANSWER: *United States, Canada, Japan and Mexico*

TODAY'S THOUGHT:

"I won't play for a penny less than fifteen-hundred dollars."
—*Honus Wagner*, after rejecting a $2,000 salary

HISTORY:

On this date in 1955 Hall of Fame shortstop Honus Wagner died at the age of eighty-one. Exactly 30 years later another Hall of Famer, Burleigh Grimes, the last legal spitball pitcher, passed away at ninety-two.

BIRTHDAYS:

Jocko Conlan, 1899; Tony Lazzeri, 1903; Stan Hack, 1909; Larry Bowa, 1945; Steve Bedrosian, 1957; Kevin Appier, 1967; Jose Contreras, 1971

TRIVIA:

Burleigh Grimes never shaved on days that he was scheduled to pitch because the slippery elm he chewed to increase saliva irritated his skin. As a result, he earned the nickname, "Ol' Stubblebeard."

QUIZ:

When this shortstop won the NL Gold Glove in 1993 he broke a string of thirteen consecutive Gold Gloves for another National League shortstop. Name both.

ANSWER: *Jay Bell of the Pirates beat out perennial winner Ozzie Smith of the Cardinals.*

TODAY'S THOUGHT:

"I've come to the conclusion that the two most important things in life are good friends and a good bullpen." —*Bob Lemon*

HISTORY:

On this date in 1995 the Yankees acquired first baseman Tino Martinez from the Seattle Mariners to replace the retiring Don Mattingly. Martinez would play an integral role for a Yankees team that won three straight World Series from 1998 to 2000.

BIRTHDAYS:

Deacon White, 1847; Bo Belinsky, 1936; Johnny Bench, 1947; Shane Mack, 1963; Tino Martinez, 1967; Eric Chavez, 1977

TRIVIA:

Don Mattingly holds the season record for most at-bats without a stolen base: 677.

EXTRA INNING:

"The reason baseball calls itself a game, I believe, is that it is too screwed up to be a business." –*Jim Bouton*

QUIZ:

What NFL coaching legend played briefly for the New York Yankees in 1919?

ANSWER: *Chicago Bears coach George Halas*

TODAY'S THOUGHT:

"Gaylord Perry and Willie McCovey should know each other like a book. They've been ex-teammates for years now."
—*Jerry Coleman*

HISTORY:

On this date in 1966 the New York Yankees traded Roger Maris to the St. Louis Cardinals for journeyman third baseman Charley Smith. Maris would play in two World Series for the Cardinals before retiring after the 1968 season.

BIRTHDAYS:

Mike Mussina, 1968; Jeff DaVanon, 1973; Reed Johnson, 1976; Vernon Wells, 1978

TRIVIA:

Roger Maris hit 275 home runs in his twelve-year career. Other than his 61 in '61, he only hit 30 or more homers twice, the year before and after his record-breaking season.

QUIZ:

When Roger Maris belted 61 homers to lead the American League in 1961, who led the National League in that category?

ANSWER: *Orlando Cepeda of the San Francisco Giants, with 46*

TODAY'S THOUGHT:

"He makes it look easy. You wish there was another league he could get called up to." —*Doc Gooden*, on Greg Maddux

HISTORY:

On this date in 1992 the Atlanta Braves signed Cy Young Award winner Greg Maddux away from the Chicago Cubs. Maddux would lead the Braves to a World Series title in 1995, eventually returning to the Cubs in 2004.

BIRTHDAYS:

Joe Kelley, 1871; Cy Seymour, 1872; Tony Batista, 1973

TRIVIA:

Maddux was the first pitcher to win four consecutive Cy Young Awards (1992 to '95), and the first pitcher to have an ERA below 1.65 in back-to-back seasons (1.56 in '94 and 1.63 in '95).

EXTRA INNING:

"I like Doug DeCinces and all, but I got tired of talking to him all the time." –*Terry Harper*, on the language barrier playing in Japan

QUIZ:

Dizzy Dean pitched for what St. Louis team?

ANSWER: *If you said the Cardinals, you're only half right. Dean also pitched four innings for the St. Louis Browns on September 28, 1947.*

TODAY'S THOUGHT:

"If I ever decide to do a book, I've already got the title - *The Bases Were Loaded and So Was I.*" —*Jim Fregosi*

HISTORY:

On this date in 1971 the Mets traded twenty-four year-old pitcher Nolan Ryan and three other prospects to the California Angels for six-time all-star shortstop Jim Fregosi. Fregosi would be traded to Texas in less than two years after hitting .233 with New York.

BIRTHDAYS:

Jimmy Johnston, 1889; Joe Mays, 1975; Dan Wheeler, 1977; Victor Diaz, 1981

TRIVIA:

Jim Fregosi became the manager of the Blue Jays in 1999 after previous skipper Tim Johnson lied about his experience in the Vietnam War to motivate his players. Johnson trained Vietnam-bound recruits, but never actually served in Southeast Asia.

QUIZ:

What major league team changed its name for political reasons as a result of the Korean War?

ANSWER: *The Cincinnati Reds, who feared people would associate them with the Communists, changed their name to Cincinnati Redlegs.*

TODAY'S THOUGHT:

"I never knew what Joe Dimaggio looked like until I roomed with him. All I ever saw was the back of his uniform after I threw a pitch." —*Lefty Gomez*

HISTORY:

On this date in 1951 the Yankee Clipper, Joe DiMaggio, called it a career. And what a career: a .325 batting average, 361 home runs, three MVP Awards, and, oh yes, that 56-game hitting streak. DiMaggio entered the Hall of Fame in 1955.

BIRTHDAYS:

Charley Radbourn, 1854; Jay Bell, 1965; Joe Blanton, 1980

TRIVIA:

The actual playing time in a 2-1/2 hour baseball game has been clocked at 9 minutes, 55 seconds.

QUIZ:

In 1984, in the longest game in American League history, the White Sox defeated the Brewers, 7-6. What player hit the winning home run for Chicago in the game's twenty-fifth inning?

ANSWER: *Harold Baines put an end to the eight hour, six minute contest.*

TODAY'S THOUGHT:

"It is more profitable to have a team that is in contention for most of the season but finishes about fourth. A team like that will draw well enough during the first part of the season to show a profit for the year, and you don't have to give the players raises when they don't win." —*Connie Mack*

HISTORY:

On this date in 1933 Athletics owner Connie Mack sold pitcher Lefty Grove and two other players to the Boston Red Sox for $125,000. Grove was the team's top winner for the past five seasons, including a 31-4 record in 1931.

BIRTHDAY:

Tully Sparks, 1874; Ralph Garr, 1945; Gorman Thomas, 1950; Orlando Hudson, 1977

TRIVIA:

In 1932, when the A's played a one-game series in Cleveland, Mack brought just two pitchers on the trip to save train fare. After his starter was pulled in the first inning, knuckleballer Ed Rommel was forced to pitch the rest of the way, which turned out to be 17 innings. He gave up 33 hits but won the game, 18-17.

QUIZ:

What two animals have served as mascots for the Oakland Athletics?

ANSWER: *An elephant and a mule*

TODAY'S THOUGHT:

"A baseball park is the one place where a man's wife doesn't mind his getting excited over somebody else's curves."
—*Brendan Francis*

HISTORY:

On this date in 1996 the Toronto Blue Jays signed Roger Clemens to a three-year contract worth $24.75 million. His career thought to be on the decline by Boston, Clemens proved his former club wrong by winning back-to-back Cy Young Awards in 1997 and 1998 with Toronto.

BIRTHDAYS:

Larry Doby, 1923; Fergie Jenkins, 1942

TRIVIA:

A's owner Charlie Finley once offered his then eighteen year-old pitcher Vida Blue $10,000 to change his name to "True" Blue. Blue declined, stating his first name Vida meant "life."

EXTRA INNING:

"Frank Howard is so big that he wasn't born; he was founded." –*Jim Murray*

QUIZ:

Don Gullett of the Reds gave up the 660th, and final, homer hit by Willie Mays. Which Hall of Fame pitcher surrendered his first?

ANSWER: *Warren Spahn*

TODAY'S THOUGHT:

"Five." —*Alex Johnson*, when asked to explain the difference in his hitting two home runs one year to seven the next

HISTORY:

On this date in 1980 and 1985 baseball lost two former MVPs. In 1980, Elston Howard died of a heart ailment at the age of 51. Howard was the first African-American to be voted the American League's Most Valuable Player Award in 1963. Five years later, Roger Maris, also 51, died of lymphatic cancer. Maris, the player who broke Babe Ruth's 34-year old home run record, was the AL MVP in 1960 and '61.

BIRTHDAYS:

Lefty Tyler, 1889; Bill Buckner, 1949; Craig Biggio, 1965; Scott Hatteberg, 1969; Billy Koch, 1974

TRIVIA:

Elston Howard invented the "donut", the circular lead weight with a rubber shell used by on-deck hitters.

QUIZ:

Who was the first Yankee to lead the American League in home runs since Roger Maris in 1961?

ANSWER: *Graig Nettles, with thirty-two in 1976*

TODAY'S THOUGHT:

"If he'd just tip his cap once, he could be elected mayor of Boston in five minutes." —*Eddie Collins*, on Ted Williams

HISTORY:

On this date in 1980 outfielder Dave Winfield became the highest-paid player in major league history when he left the Padres for a 10-year, $15 million contract with the New York Yankees. The Hall of Famer would play for four other teams after spending eight years with the Yankees.

BIRTHDAYS:

Jim Leyland, 1944; Mo Vaughn, 1967; Aaron Miles, 1976

TRIVIA:

Seat 21, row 37, section 42 is called "The Red Seat," commemorating the longest homer ever hit in Fenway Park. That was a 502-foot shot by Ted Williams in 1946.

EXTRA INNING:

"Charles Finley is a self-made man who worships his creator." –*Jim Murray*

QUIZ:

Can you name the two brothers who were battery mates for the Red Sox from 1934 to '36?

ANSWER: *Wes and Rick Ferrell (Wes was the pitcher, Rick the catcher)*

TODAY'S THOUGHT:

"Me and George and Billy are two of a kind." —*Mickey Rivers*, on his relationship with George Steinbrenner and Billy Martin

HISTORY:

On this date in 1983 Yankees owner George Steinbrenner hired Yogi Berra after firing manager Billy Martin for the third time. After finishing in third place in 1984, Berra was then fired just sixteen games into the next season and replaced by...Billy Martin.

BIRTHDAYS:

Mike Flanagan, 1951; Billy Ripken, 1964

TRIVIA:

Short-tempered Billy Martin was fired by Steinbrenner as Yankees manager for the second time when, in 1979, he punched out marshmallow salesman Joseph Cooper in a Minnesota bar following a baseball argument.

EXTRA INNING:

"Candlestick was built on the water. It should have built under it."
–*Roger Maris*

QUIZ:

What was Billy Martin's real name?

ANSWER: *Alfred Manuel Pesano*

TODAY'S THOUGHT:

"I'm starting to hate talking about the Yankees...They're wasting my time...I don't believe in damn curses. Wake up the damn Bambino and have me face him. Maybe I'll drill him in the ass." —*Pedro Martinez,* on the Yankees-Red Sox rivalry

HISTORY:

On this date in 2004 the New York Mets signed former Red Sox ace Pedro Martinez to a four-year deal worth $53 million. Martinez posted a 117-37 record in seven seasons with Boston, winning two Cy Young Awards and one World Series ring.

BIRTHDAYS:

Bob Ojeda, 1957; Chase Utley, 1978; Alex Cintron, 1978

TRIVIA:

Before the 2004 season, Pedro Martinez befriended Nelson De la Rosa, an actor from the Dominican Republic who's less than three feet tall. De la Rosa served as Boston's good luck charm during its championship run.

QUIZ:

Who is the only player to hit a home run in his lone at-bat in the World Series?

ANSWER: *Jim Mason of the New York Yankees, who hit a home run in game three of the 1976 World Series against the Reds*

TODAY'S THOUGHT:

"Well, that kind of puts a damper even on a Yankee win."
—*Phil Rizzuto*, upon hearing the news that the pope had died in 1978

HISTORY:

On this date in 1956 Phil Rizzuto, less than three months after being released as a player by New York, signed on with the Yankees as a radio-TV announcer. He would go on to call games for 40 years.

BIRTHDAYS:

Ty Cobb, 1886; Bill Skowron, 1930; Joe Randa, 1969

TRIVIA:

Rizzuto was the first mystery guest on the long-running television program *What's My Line?* when the show premiered in February of 1950. Between 1956 and 1957, he would return for three more appearances as a guest panelist.

QUIZ:

After Mel Allen's death in 1996, what former baseball player temporarily replaced him as the host of *This Week in Baseball?*

ANSWER: *Ozzie Smith*

TODAY'S THOUGHT:

"I grew up in an age when we prayed the Cubs and White Sox would merge so we would only have one bad team in Chicago."
—*Tom Dreesen*, comedian

HISTORY:

On this date in 2003 that infamous baseball deflected by Cubs fan Steve Bartman in Game Six of the 2003 NLCS was purchased for $106,600 by the managing partner of Harry Caray's Restaurant Group in Chicago. The ball was then destroyed in 2004 as part of a toast to Harry on his birthday.

BIRTHDAYS:

Ford Frick, 1894; Al Kaline, 1934; Bill Wegman, 1962; Russell Branyan, 1975

TRIVIA:

Home plate was square until 1900, when it was made five-sided to help umpires call balls and strikes.

EXTRA INNING:

"Rick Sutcliffe was the rookie of the year in his first year." –*Ralph Kiner*

QUIZ:

As a twenty year-old rookie with the Texas Rangers, Sammy Sosa hit his first career home run off what future Hall of Famer?

ANSWER: *Boston's Roger Clemens, in 1989*

TODAY'S THOUGHT:

"Two grand slams in a week - man, that's seven or eight ribbies right there." —*Bill Madlock*

HISTORY:

On this date in 1926 Rogers Hornsby was traded from the Cardinals to the New York Giants for Frankie Frisch and Jimmy Ring. After twelve years in St. Louis, Hornsby would play for three different teams in the next three years.

BIRTHDAYS:

Branch Rickey, 1881; Gabby Hartnett, 1900; Spud Davis, 1904; Oscar Gamble, 1949; Cecil Cooper, 1949; Aubrey Huff, 1976; David DeJesus, 1979; David Wright, 1982

TRIVIA:

Hornsby, a two-time Triple Crown winner, became the first big leaguer to connect for an extra-inning, pinch-hit grand slam. He did it in 1931 when his Cubs defeated the Braves in eleven innings.

QUIZ:

In the 1999 NL Championship Series, what player became the first to hit a "grand slam single?"

ANSWER: *Robin Ventura - In the fifteenth inning of game five against the Braves, the Mets' Ventura hit a walk-off grand slam, but never got past first base after being mobbed by his team-mates.*

TODAY'S THOUGHT:

"If it was that easy, Billy Graham would hit .400." —*Chris Sabo*, on Marge Schott suggesting the Reds try praying to end their losing streak

HISTORY:

On this date in 1984 Marge Schott purchased controlling interest of the Cincinnati Reds for a reported $12 million. In doing so, she became the first female owner to buy a baseball team, rather than inherit it.

BIRTHDAYS:

Josh Gibson, 1911; Dave Kingman, 1948; Tom Henke, 1957; Andy Van Slyke, 1960; Roger McDowell, 1960; Dustin Hermanson, 1972; LaTroy Hawkins, 1972

TRIVIA:

In 1996, Schott opted not to pay for the ticker service which provides scores of out-of-town games for fans in the ballpark. Schott reasoned that Cincinnati fans simply had no interest in games not involving the Reds.

QUIZ:

In 2000, the Reds became the first team to go an entire 162-game season without enduring what negative scoreboard consequence?

ANSWER: *They went the entire season without being shut out.*

TODAY'S THOUGHT:

"The first pitch to Tucker Ashford is grounded into left field. No, wait a minute. It's ball one. Low and outside." —*Jerry Coleman*

HISTORY:

On this date in 1953 the newly relocated St. Louis Browns officially became the Baltimore Orioles. The team would draw over one million fans in its first season in Baltimore.

BIRTHDAYS:

Connie Mack, 1862; Matty Alou, 1938; Steve Carlton, 1944; Steve Garvey, 1948; Lonnie Smith, 1955; Jason Lane, 1976

TRIVIA:

A baseball that landed in fair territory and bounced into the stands was counted as a home run until 1931, when the Baseball Rules Committee decided it should be a ground-rule double instead.

EXTRA INNING:

"The kid is the greatest proof of reincarnation. Nobody could get that stupid in one lifetime." –*Joe McCarthy*, after a player was thrown out trying to steal home with one out

QUIZ:

Who was the first player to homer for his 3,000th career major league hit?

ANSWER: *Wade Boggs, as a member of the Tampa Bay Devil Rays*

TODAY'S THOUGHT:

"Not really - they lean towards cash." —*Bill Veeck*, when asked if free agents leaned toward big cities

HISTORY:

On this date in 1975 a ruling by arbitrator Peter Seitz made pitchers Dave McNally and Andy Messersmith the first true free agents in Major League Baseball history. The landmark decision led to the agreement that all players would become eligible for free agency after six seasons.

BIRTHDAYS:

Jerry Koosman, 1942; Brad Lidge, 1976; Shawn Chacon, 1977; Victor Martinez, 1978; Hanley Ramirez, 1983

TRIVIA:

Catfish Hunter was technically the first free agent in 1974. After A's owner Charlie Finley failed to make a $50,000 payment on the pitcher's life insurance, an arbitrator declared Hunter's contract breached, thus freeing him to sign on with another team. Hunter signed with the Yankees.

QUIZ:

True or false? In 1975, Hunter was the subject of the Bob Dylan song, *Catfish*.

ANSWER: *True*

TODAY'S THOUGHT:

"He went from Cy Young to sayonara in a year."—*Graig Nettles*, on Sparky Lyle

HISTORY:

On this date in 1967 Boston Red Sox pitcher Jim Lonborg tore ligaments in his left knee while skiing at Lake Tahoe. Lonborg, the Cy Young Award winner that year, pitched 12 more years but was not as effective. Lonborg never won more than ten games in his final four years in Boston.

BIRTHDAY:

Kevin Millwood, 1974

TRIVIA:

San Diego pitcher Adam Eaton missed a start in 2001 when he accidentally stabbed himself in the stomach trying to take the shrink-wrap off a DVD with a knife.

QUIZ:

In 1983, what pitcher's ERA of 3.66 was the highest of any Cy Young Award winner?

ANSWER: *LaMarr Hoyt, who went 24-10 with the White Sox that year*

TODAY'S THOUGHT:

"I may not have been the greatest Yankee to put on the uniform but I was the proudest." *—epitaph on Billy Martin's headstone*

HISTORY:

On this date in 1989 Billy Martin, who played on four World Series championship teams with the New York Yankees and was a five-time manager of the club, died at age 61 in a motor vehicle accident near his home in Binghamton, New York.

BIRTHDAYS:

Pud Galvin, 1856; Ben Chapman, 1908; Nellie Fox, 1927; Rickey Henderson, 1958; Willy Tavares, 1981

TRIVIA:

The bases in baseball measure 15 inches by 15 inches - excluding home, of course.

EXTRA INNING:

"Ice is for mixed drinks." –*Warren Spahn*, asked if he put ice on a sore arm

QUIZ:

Who won a Manager of the Year Award with three different teams?

ANSWER: *Tony La Russa, with the White Sox in 1983, the A's in 1988 and 1992, and the Cardinals in 2002*

TODAY'S THOUGHT:

"The President took all the news very calmly. I'd seen Enos Slaughter get more upset about an umpire say 'Strike two' than Gerald Ford did when he realized he wasn't going to win a presidential election." —*Joe Garagiola*

HISTORY:

On this date in 1974 President Gerald Ford signed into law a bill declaring the Little League officially open to girls. A series of lawsuits had challenged the organization's boys-only rule.

BIRTHDAYS:

Stu Miller, 1927; Carlton Fisk, 1947; Chris Chambliss, 1948; Ozzie Smith, 1954

TRIVIA:

When Cardinals' pitcher Jason Marquis and Red Sox catcher Jason Varitek squared off against each other in the 2004 World Series, it was the first time in major league history that Little League World Series participants faced each other as pitcher and batter in the Fall Classic.

QUIZ:

This team won 111 games to set an American League record. What was the team and in what year was it done?

ANSWER: *The Cleveland Indians, in 1954*

TODAY'S THOUGHT:

"If you can't stand the heat, get out of the chicken."
—*The San Diego Chicken*

HISTORY:

On this date in 1994 Julio Franco and Pete Incaviglia signed contracts to play in Japan for the Chiba Lotte Marines. The team was led by Bobby Valentine, the first American manager in professional Japanese baseball.

BIRTHDAYS:

Roy White, 1943; Jim Leyritz, 1963; Dean Palmer, 1968

TRIVIA:

The San Diego Chicken, a mascot played by Ted Giannoulas, was named one of the 100 most powerful people in sports for the twentieth century by *The Sporting News.*

EXTRA INNING:

"I had a lot of no-hitters in the minors. They were games when I didn't hit anybody." –*Jim Kern*

QUIZ:

In 1995, what major league mascot gained national attention when he broke his ankle crashing into an outfield wall at the Kingdome?

ANSWER: *The Mariner Moose, who hurt himself while being towed on inline skates behind an ATV*

TODAY'S THOUGHT:

"The Houston Astros are the youngest team in the National League if you judge by age." —*Don Drysdale*

HISTORY:

On this date in 1994 the Houston Astros and San Diego Padres completed a huge twelve-player trade. Among the players Houston obtained were outfielder Derek Bell and infielder Ricky Gutiérrez. The Padres received third baseman Ken Caminiti, outfielder Steve Finley, and four other players.

BIRTHDAYS:

Ted Lyons, 1900; Tommy Bridges, 1906; Benny Agbayani, 1971; B.J. Ryan, 1975; Bill Hall, 1979

TRIVIA:

The Orioles and Yankees made history in 1954 with a monumental 17-player deal that took several days to complete. Featured in the swap were pitchers Bob Turley and Don Larsen, who were sent to New York, and catcher Gus Triandos, who went to Baltimore.

QUIZ:

In 1990, the Houston Astros traded thirty-seven year-old reliever Larry Andersen to the Boston Red Sox for what Double-A prospect?

ANSWER: *Jeff Bagwell*

TODAY'S THOUGHT:

"When I first saw Yankee Stadium I thought, 'Boy this place is big.'" —*Yogi Berra*

HISTORY:

On this date in 2002 Cinergy Field, home to the Cincinnati Reds since 1970, was demolished. The site became the western concourse of Great American Ball Park, the Reds' new home in 2003.

BIRTHDAYS:

Devon White, 1962; Richie Sexson, 1974; Jaret Wright, 1975; Jack Wilson, 1977

TRIVIA:

The baseball phrase "around the horn" comes from the nautical term for a ship sailing between the Atlantic and the Pacific before the Panama Canal was completed.

EXTRA INNING:

"He can pitch when he's relaxed, and he'll be happy and relaxed here. If he isn't, we'll kill him." –*John Kruk*, on the Phillies acquiring Mark Davis

QUIZ:

What stadium played host to the major league's biggest crowd ever?

ANSWER: *Los Angeles Memorial Coliseum - In 1959, a crowd of 93,103 watched an exhibition game between the Dodgers and Yankees played in honor of Roy Campanella.*

TODAY'S THOUGHT:

"Baseball's a very simple game. All you have to do is sit on your ass, spit tobacco, and nod at the stupid things your manager says." —*Bill Lee*

HISTORY:

On this date in 1907 The Mills Commission reported that "the first scheme for playing baseball, according to the best evidence obtainable to date, was devised by Abner Doubleday in Cooperstown, N.Y. in 1839." The committee, headed by Albert Spalding and Abraham Mills, was convinced by the testimony of Abner Graves, a childhood friend of Doubleday's.

BIRTHDAYS:

Sandy Koufax, 1935; A.J. Pierzynski, 1976

TRIVIA:

Abner Doubleday was a US Army officer and Union general in the American Civil War. He fired the first shot in defense of Fort Sumter.

QUIZ:

The inventor of the box score and author of one of baseball's first rule books was dubbed the "Father of Baseball." Name him.

ANSWER: *Henry Chadwick - He was the first writer to be inducted into Cooperstown.*

TODAY'S THOUGHT:

"Any time you have an opportunity to make a difference in this world and you don't, then you are wasting your time on Earth." —*Roberto Clemente*

HISTORY:

On this date in 1972 thirty-eight year-old Roberto Clemente died in a plane crash while delivering relief supplies to earthquake victims in Managua, Nicaragua. The cargo plane, which departed from San Juan Airport in Puerto Rico, crashed shortly after takeoff.

BIRTHDAYS:

King Kelly, 1857; Jim Tracy, 1955; Esteban Loaiza, 1971; Chris Reitsma, 1977

TRIVIA:

The 2006 movie *Chasing 3,000* tells the story of two brothers who travel across country to see Clemente get his 3,000th hit.

EXTRA INNING:

"A waist is a terrible thing to mind." –*Terry Forster*, Braves pitcher

QUIZ:

With whom does Clemente share the record for the most career games played as a Pittsburgh Pirate?

ANSWER: *Honus Wagner - Both played in 2,433 games with Pittsburgh.*

"AS I SAY, I NEVER FEEL MORE AT HOME IN AMERICA THAN AT A BALL GAME BE IT IN PARK OR IN SANDLOT. BEYOND THIS I KNOW NOT AND DARE NOT."

—Robert Frost